The Standout Agent

Cynthia DeLuca

www.CynthiaDeLuca.com

No financial guarantees or warrants of any kind are made from this material.

ISBN: 978-1-7326592-3-0

This book is dedicated to the countless people who have helped shape my career in real estate.

To my very first broker, the late Charlie Barry, who taught me patience in real estate.

To my first sales manager, Tom Milton, who taught me to read every line of the contract, over and over again until I had it memorized. *He who knows the rules of the game wins every time.*

To the agents who trusted me to be their fearless leader and broker. You know how much I love you and consider you family. Thank you for the experiences, the friendships, and the trust you put in me.

To my attorney, Darren Elkind, who taught me so much about liability and best practices and to stay calm.

To my door-knocking partner, Bob Barker, who always kept me accountable.

To my community partner, Terry Bailey, who always found ways to make our community a better place through non-profits, time, and love.

To my real estate sister and sales manager, Beverley Hibbert, who allowed me to teach her about real estate and, in return, she taught me how to be a woman of God.

To my students and coaching clients, who have shown me that the steps in this book, when practiced consistently, can yield exponential results.

For everyone who worked with me in various roles, from real estate agent to broker to leadership positions to speaker and author, you have each uniquely formed me into who I am. Thank you for your presence in my life.

To my family. Without the unconditional support from my husband and children, so much in my life would not have been possible.

Thank you all, from the bottom of my heart.

Contents

Introduction

I bought a house. Not just any house, but my first house. I wish I could say this is when my love for real estate began, but it wasn't. It was just 2 ½ months after I turned 18 years old. I was juggling college and a job, plus now I became an "adult" with bills. Real bills. I wish I could say I had a great experience with a real estate professional, but I didn't. I bought a For Sale by Owner with no agent involved. I wish I could say I had dropped out of college and began my fabulous real estate career at 18, but I didn't. I often think about how much more successful I would be had I started earlier, but that first house at the time, seemed like no big deal. It was just a house.

Fast forward some years later. I outgrew that house, sold it and bought a new one, at the same time, or what we called then a simultaneous closing. I needed the proceeds from the first sale to pay for the down payment for my new purchase, and literally we used to do this all at the same signing session, simultaneously. I did this simultaneous closing and move all with a 1-year-old and a 2-week-old baby.

That's when I discovered my love.

I had a real estate professional help me sell my first house along with assisting me on the purchase of the next one. Virginia was her name, and she remains my friend to this day. She made the entire process seem so smooth, so easy, so carefree.

After the move and settling in, I needed a change. Not excited at my current career, I started researching a real estate career. Gosh, who wouldn't want to meet nice people all day, look at beautiful homes and make beaucoup money in the meantime? Or at least, that's what it seemed like to me. And probably many of you reading this book as well.

Once I made the plunge into real estate, I quickly realized, this is not all fun and games. Less than 6 months into my new career, in which all expenses had been charged on my credit card, I figured out that I better figure this business out or get out!

Trust me, if I can make it in this business, anyone can!

I did everything wrong in the beginning. Literally, everything! I was shy and didn't know how to talk to people. I wasn't confident and lost opportunities for business. I was young and looked even younger, and customers noticed my youth as a disadvantage.

If I can make it, and not just survive, but <u>thrive</u> in this industry, you can too!

Even if you know nothing, you have come to the right place. In the few hours it will take you to read this book, you will learn the tips and tools needed to become a successful real estate entrepreneur.

To make this process as easy as possible for you, this book has been divided into four distinct sections. Each provides valuable information for new and budding real estate agents along with anyone looking to catapult their existing real estate business to the next level.

The first section is all about you. Since you are the core of the business, it is critical to start with you.

This begins with setting a realistic budget for starting or re-starting your career. It also involves deciding how much time you must commit to this venture.

Creating *You, Inc.* is about understanding why this career is so important you. It is about setting the right goals (the right way). It requires developing a system of accountability and truly realizing your worth.

In this first section, we also talk about the importance of identifying and researching your competition, so you know how you are unique. How you stand out. I will also explain the importance of playing hard to get. That's right. It may seem counterintuitive, but you will understand why I suggest that you do this shortly.

Starting to feel overwhelmed? Not to worry. You don't have to go through this alone. Part of becoming a profitable real estate venture involves adding others to your team, such as a mentor or a partner.

In the second section, we dive deeper into how to develop what I call "Bigwig Status." This is where you go from a fledgling real estate agent to one of your area's biggest players.

In part, this requires setting up multiple databases. Why more than one? I'll explain that momentarily but suffice it to say that each one pays dividends in different ways, so it's necessary to treat them differently.

I'll also provide other ways to be a true star in the real estate field. For instance, you will learn "the power of donuts" and how to use social media to your advantage. We'll also talk about the importance of your resume, how to monitor trends, and ways to literally multiply your exposure.

How do you make all of this happen seamlessly? That's the purpose of section three because this is where we get into the nitty-gritty—the nuts and bolts—of creating a profitable real estate business.

In this section, I will share with you the systems I've used to create an ever-growing list of buyers and sellers. Some of the things we will go over include how to create the right vendor teams and how to fire your customers. (Yes, you may have to do this from time to time. But there is a way to do it that won't hurt your reputation.)

I'll also reveal the secrets behind creating a listing that sells. Hint: it involves using online marketing to your advantage and the key to setting up the right open house for that listing. It even includes door knocking!

In the last section, we talk about the ballast effect, or creating balance. We will go over how to get the most out of your hours worked and factors to consider when deciding your hours of operation. You will learn how to make the most of state and national conventions (ready for a vacation?) as well as a few ways to create a healthy level of work-life balance.

This may seem like an overwhelming amount of information, but we will go through it all one small step at a time. This allows you to digest it in a way that makes it easier to understand. It also enables you to create a top-notch real estate business right from day one.

Are you ready to take this journey into what is sure to be an amazing real estate career? Good! Let's begin by taking a closer look at the one person who can make this goal a reality: YOU.

PS-Everything in this book I have personally experienced and done. I would never ask you to do anything that I didn't know firsthand if it worked. These strategies have worked for countless others, and now I'm excited to share them with you.

Before You Get Started…

This book is meant to bring you new ideas and challenge you. Though not required, it is extremely helpful to have an accountability partner work through this book at the same time as you. Is there someone in your office you can ask to also be a Standout agent, someone on your team, a mentor, broker, or even your spouse? With someone by your side, it will ensure you commit to making these changes and start or improve your real estate career immediately.

So, find someone and ask them today. They don't even have to be in your market area. Get them this book and get started together…

Section 1
You

Chapter 1
Focus on You

"The world is before you and you need not take it or leave it as it was when you came in."
James Baldwin, Writer and Playwright

You, Inc.

You, Inc. That is what you are as a real estate agent. You are a company of one, self-employed and in charge of yourself. So, think back to the very first day you became a real estate agent. The day when you took your test, and you received your notice that you had passed. Congratulations! Such an exciting day. But what exactly does that mean?

For me, I had 2 kids under the age of 2. I had taken time off work to start my family, but was urgently wanting to get back to adulthood. Changing diapers all day was not my idea of fun. So, I interviewed at several companies in my current field, advertising. All had strict rules of showing up at 8am and leaving at 5pm. Time off was not a thing until I "earned" my PTO days. I didn't see how my current career would work out with a family. I needed more freedom, an adjustable schedule to work around my babies for when they were sick, when they had field trips, etc. Besides, Virginia made real estate look easy. I decided to make a change. Real estate, here I come.

After taking a 7 day cram course for my pre-license class, I locked myself in my bedroom to have some time to study alone. That next Tuesday, I went to a testing center and took my state exam. I waited for my results to print, which seemed like it took an eternity, I remember thinking, *what if I don't pass? What do I do next? What if I do pass? Then what?*

The testing clerk handed me the printed results, and there it was…P-A-S-S. But what does that mean?

Forget about real estate for a moment. We could have chosen any path we wanted. We could have opened any type of business we desired. Let's think about opening a business for a moment, but NOT a real estate business. When opening a business, many decide to do a business plan, create a budget, understand the competition, and know their product inside and out…better than anyone else. You have a vision and a plan for what your company looks like. Do you understand who your client is going to be, your target customer? Who needs your product the most?

Let's take a look at the different kinds of businesses we could decide to open.

- A restaurant
- A coffee shop
- A bookstore
- A shoe store
- A dry cleaner

How much do you think it would cost to open any one of these businesses? By the time you take into account all the things you need to get started, all the things to get "your doors open," it could easily cost at least $100,000 to open when all is said and done.

Let's also think about what you need when you open a business.

- A business plan
- A name
- A logo
- A website
- A location
- Insurance
- Possible employees
- Inventory
- Build-out of your new space
- Deposits for water, power, and other utilities
- Social media sites
- Cash registers
- Benefits for employees
- Marketing pieces

The list goes on and on. Now start adding up these expenses. You'll see it's easily $100,000. And that's before considering your ongoing marketing efforts needed to *keep* your doors open.

Now, back to real estate.

Think back to that day, that really exciting day that you passed your real estate exam. You became *You, Inc.* You became your own business. What's the difference?

The difference is that you didn't incur most of these expenses. When you picked a brokerage, a lot of these items "came with" your broker. Your brokerage already had a location, a website, and possibly already even had a ringing phone.

Let's assume you didn't spend $100,000 opening your real estate company. So, what did you spend to open *You, Inc*? Probably not much, or less than $5,000. Five-grand, to open a full fledge business with the possibility of huge returns! Let's consider today the re-opening of your business: *You Inc*. You are fortunate that you have the opportunity to start all over again, without spending your life's savings. If you don't have a lot of money to spend on your business, then you need to have the *time* to spend.

What could you do with your time?

- Farming
- Door knocking
- Open houses
- In-person networking

- Social media networking
- Blogging
- Five a day (more on this later)

The list goes on and on. And we will cover so much of this in this book, and more.

If you're happy with your business the way that it is—and you're not willing to make some changes—you should probably stop reading right now. Otherwise, welcome to the grand opening of *You, Inc!*

Time Versus Money

When opening *You, Inc.*, the one thing you must decide upfront is how much time and money you have (and want) to dedicate to your new business.

How many hours per week do you have available to meet with clients, market your services, and tend to all of your other business needs? How much time can you spare without overwhelming yourself, so this business helps you accomplish your dreams versus becoming a nightmare?

Additionally, what times of day are you more available than others? For instance, if you have children, is your goal to work during the day while they are in school? Are weekends good for you because your spouse will be home and able to look after them?

If a client wants to meet with you outside these times, do you have someone who can watch your kids, sometimes on a moment's notice? Are you willing to show a listing at night or on a holiday weekend?

These are all schedule-related factors that should be considered upfront. The more realistic you are with your availability, the easier it is to plan a business that fits into your current lifestyle.

Also, consider how much money you have available to invest. Although you don't need $100,000 to begin to sell houses, there are some start-up costs to think about.

One is your website. Some sites enable you to create your own, but if you don't have the time or the desire to learn how to use them, you may be further ahead by paying someone else to create your site for you.

Another cost is marketing. Granted, social media sites are free—unless you purchase an ad—and a good way to get the word out about your business and listings. But if you want a wider reach, you may need to invest in more traditional marketing methods. This includes direct mailings, newspaper ads, and a spot on local radio stations.

There are also costs associated with your listings. You'll need a good, high-quality printer to create flyers with pictures of the property and all of its specs. You'll also need to purchase the "For Sale" signs that will be placed in front of the home or building, indicating that the property is available and containing your contact information.

How much money do you have to invest in these types of items to get your new business off the ground? Not that you must splurge and build the best website possible, buying only the top advertising mediums, and getting thousands of signs made up, because you don't. But you will need some cash right now to get the ball rolling on some of these items. So, it's a consideration that you need to think about when planning *You, Inc.*

Looking at your budget, how much cash do you have to put into your new real estate venture? It's best to be on the conservative side so you don't overextend too much, putting you in a pinch.

If you have a spouse or significant other, talk this over with them. Make sure he or she knows how much you need to begin your career. This prevents any misunderstandings from occurring, such as you taking out more than they thought. It's best if you're on the same page.

My first year, I spent more money than I made. Between marketing expenses, gas, advertising, etc, I lost money in my venture. But don't most new businesses lose money their first year, only to come back stronger the second year?

What's Your Why?

Before starting any business venture, you must ask yourself why? Why did you choose real estate? Why did you decide that this is the right time in your life to be a real estate agent? Why?

Some people choose this career because they want more control over their time. Others join because the sky is the limit with income. Still, others decide to take this route because they have a strong desire to help people and they want to be in relationships with people. The reasons are endless.

Your why needs to be the driving factor behind everything you do. You must scribe it and keep it handy so that when you have tough days—and you *will* have tough days—you can always go back and refer to it.

It's also important to go back and refer to your why when you prepare your goals. Goals keep you on track and are very important to make sure you achieve the life you want, the career you want, and the success you want, however you define it. Your why is the entire focus of your goals.

Think big. *What is your why?*

In an attempt to not re-create the wheel here, I would strongly encourage you to read the book *Start With Why* by Simon Sinek. It will definitely bring clarity to this question if you are struggling with the answer.

On a side note, I have an entire list of recommended reading on my website. If you like to read or listen to audiobooks, check out my list at www.CynthiaDeLuca.com. Feel free to submit any books you'd like to add to the list!

Okay, back to the question at hand. Pause your reading and take a moment to think about your why. Jot down the reasons you want to get involved in real estate. What does this particular career stand to offer you?

My Why is: ______________________________

____

Set Your Goals

When I entered the real estate industry, I had never set a goal before in my life. At least not formally. Sure, I had things I wanted to do and things I wanted to accomplish, but I never really went through the act of goal setting. It is life-changing! I mean *real* life-changing.

Setting goals can help you understand the daily activities, weekly activities, monthly activities, and so on that you need to be doing to achieve the life you want in the timeframe you want.

It's often said that you need to set goals on an annual basis. I tend to think a little differently about this. I like to set long-term goals and work my way back.

For instance, think 20 years in the future. What do you imagine your life to be like at that point? Do you want to have rental properties, a certain amount of money in the bank or just be debt-free?

Do you want to travel or imagine a life of relaxation? Are you still working, or do you need income from passive investments to provide for your living? Where do you see yourself in 20 years?

After you figure out exactly where you want to be in 20 years, let's start breaking this down backward. If you were to be at your desired level in 20 years, where do you need to be in 10 years? Once you figure out where you need to be in 10 years, break that down to where you need to be in five years.

Once you figure out where you need to be in five years, break that down to where you need to be each year between now and then. Following with the process of working backward makes annual goal-setting a breeze. When you look at the big picture, the end result will tell you what you need to do to get there.

One mistake that I see a lot of real estate agents make is that they are so consumed by their career and business that they totally forget about taking care of themselves. Goals need to be all-inclusive. They can't just be for your business, but also need to be for yourself, your personal time, your health, your well-being, your family, and everything in between. Goals should be all-encompassing for your entire life. Keep this in mind as we move forward.

Pause here and let's go through the activity. Where do you want to be in 20 years?

Now, break that down to where you want to be in 10 years. Write down your answers.

Let's break this down a bit further and write down where you need to be in five years.

____
____
____
____
____
____
____
____
____
____
____

Where do you have to be each year for the next five years to hit this goal?

____
____
____
____
____
____
____
____
____
____
____

Once you've completed this backward process, it's time to dive a little deeper into your goals. What I mean by this is that goals need to be SMART, which stands for *specific, measurable, achievable, relevant, and timely.*

Let's take a look at some example goals and go through the process of making them SMART.

1. A vacation to Ireland
2. A new car
3. Buy your first rental property

Looking at goal number one, to be more specific, we would need to know exactly when we will go to Ireland. Is it this year or next? How much time will we need to take off? Will it be the busy season or the offseason when we travel?

The price of travel varies greatly depending on whether you go in the busy season or slow season. It also varies the cost for you to leave your business, whether you leave during *your* busy season or *your* slow season. So, we should do some research and determine how much we think it's going to cost us to go to Ireland on our vacation.

Let's say we discovered that we need $8,000 to make this trip a reality. Now we have an approximate time of year we are going, how long we're going for, and how much it's going to cost.

Just like that, we made the goal more specific. We also made it measurable through the act of identifying the cost. Now we must work to raise the money needed.

Next, is the goal achievable? Can we bring in the money necessary before the date we want to leave? Finally, is the goal relevant and timely? Timely involves giving it a deadline. When do we need to have the money by, allowing us to reserve our flight, car, hotel room, etc.?

Do you see how going through this process makes your goal much clearer? Instead of just saying that you want to vacation in Ireland, you've now set a date, identified how much cash you need, and developed a timeline for what expenses need to be paid when. It makes it more real, right?

When you take the steps necessary to set a SMART goal, it brings that goal one step closer to becoming a reality. It gives it life. You are able to literally visualize what it will look like when you achieve it.

Some people struggle with creating SMART goals, so let's look at goal number two as another example and go through the process again. This goal involved buying a new car.

So, what kind of car do you want: a Ferrari or a Honda? Obviously, these two options vary greatly in cost. Also important to cost, is the car going to be brand new or gently used? What's your budget? All of these factors are super important to setting your goal in a way that makes it more specific *and* more measurable.

Pretty much every goal we set is going to have some type of monetary amount as a form of measurement. Whether you want to purchase something, go back to school, or get ready for retirement, all of these require that you save up some cash.

Moving through the SMART process, is the goal of getting a car achievable? Is it possible? If we want a new Ferrari within six months of entering our new real estate career but we have other expenses along the way, it might not be that achievable. Maybe down the road, in a few years, it might be a better possibility.

If you are looking for a nice reliable Honda, that is a different story. The cost would be lower, which means taking less money out of your budget. This may be a more affordable option based on your other monetary obligations.

We also need to make sure the goal is relevant. What does it have to be relevant to? Go back and review your why. This goal needs to be relevant to your vision, or your why, and your business. Does it make sense to show houses in Ferraris? I guess it depends on your market.

Are you getting the hang of this SMART goal process? Great! Let's look at one more to make sure. Goal number three is to buy your first rental property. The first step is to make it more specific.

You can buy a rental property but have a negative cash flow, which might not be exactly what you have in mind. Maybe you want to buy a rental property because you want a solid investment for your future, or you need cash flow in the here and now. Either way, determine your why for this goal, then go back and make it specific.

Do you want a single-family or do you want a duplex? Or do you want to own an apartment complex? What type of property: commercial or residential?

Next, make the goal measurable by looking at the market. Identify how much it's going to cost and, subsequently, how much will need to come out of your own pocket to make the purchase. Once you have these numbers, you can determine if the goal is achievable, if it's relevant to your why and your business, and what time frame you give yourself to make it all happen.

By the way, if your goal is to purchase a rental property, don't do it until you read my other book, *The High Heels Landlord.* It's a must read before you begin your investment career.

Ok, back to goals. Go through this process with your goals. Make sure each one is specific, measurable, achievable, relevant, and timely.

Professional Development

Professional development is really just a fancy title for making yourself smart in your profession. When you take the time to develop yourself on a professional level, it makes you better at your job. It makes you more educated and definitely elevates you above the competition.

When you're meeting with the seller discussing the listing and sale of their house, or when you're showing a property to a buyer and they want to know why they should work with you versus another real estate agent who has a ton of experience, you can set yourself apart through learning and knowledge. Remember the saying that knowledge is power. It gives you the power to win the appointment, and the customer!

I started my real estate career when I was in my 20s. I'm very fortunate to have a babyface, but I realized how much that worked against me when I was trying to win over a seller. I remember one particular seller all too well. He looked me dead in the eyes and said I was too young to sell his property and he was going to hire a different real estate agent.

At that moment, I made it my top goal to get as educated as possible in the shortest amount of time possible. I earned two real estate designations within four months and took every class I could. I read at night and researched like crazy. I needed to know more so I could beat out the competition. And that's exactly what I've been doing ever since.

Let me make one thing clear: PROFESSIONAL DEVELOPMENT NEVER ENDS. You never know it all. Things change, like every day. So, you can never, ever stop learning.

When I was starting my career, I once had a real estate agent tell me that they had over 20 years of experience in real estate and they knew exactly what they were doing. Problem was, they almost knew nothing. I knew agents who had been in the business for less than six months who knew more than this agent of 20 years.

Because this agent never took the time nor the care nor the professionalism to improve themselves to be the best they could possibly be for their customers and the transaction, they lacked imperative knowledge. They ended up getting one customer in a terrible situation which resulted in a massive lawsuit. You never know it all, especially in the real estate industry.

What classes should you take? Here are a few to consider:

- Listing Contract
- Sales Contract
- Buyer Broker Agreement
- Financing Options Update
- Ethics Training

I would recommend taking several of these classes multiple times the first two years you are in real estate. Then, once you gain a good understanding of what it's like to work in the field, take them again once every two to three years to stay up to date.

These are what I refer to as the core classes. You must know these topics inside and out to participate in the real estate industry because the person "*who knows the rules wins the game.*"

Here are some other suggested classes to increase your knowledge in the real estate industry:

- Buyer Presentation
- Seller Presentation
- Pricing and Comparative Market Analysis
- Improving Your Customer Service Through Professionalism

Every class you take accomplishes one of two things. It should either a) tell you how to make more money, or b) tell you how to save more money.

When I talk about saving money, what I'm really talking about is risk management. Risk management classes teach you how to not get sued. These are classes where you also learn how to not provide a bad customer experience. This keeps your sellers and buyers from blasting your reputation online and increases the likelihood that they will send you referrals. That's what I mean by saving money.

Many of these classes can be taken online, at a local association, or as a continuing education class that is offered by a school. The education you will receive is plentiful. You just need to get your butt in the seat and your mind focused. It is incredible how much you can improve your skills in a short amount of time with some dedication.

Pause here to do a little research and see what classes are coming up in the next four months near you. Register for them and mark them in your calendar. It is an appointment, a date set. Do not waiver, make sure you attend. This will help you be the best you can be at your business, making it well worth the time.

Business Planning

Writing a business plan can get extremely complicated, but it does not have to be. There are lots of options available to assist you in creating a draft of your business plan as a real estate agent.

A typical business plan contains a few key elements. These include:

- an executive summary
- a look at the competition
- your marketing efforts
- defining who your target customer is
- your goals
- the mission and vision of your company

- your budget

Start with the end in mind. Envision your company, *You Inc.,* and what it would look like when it is full-scale and running at its capacity. That is what you want your business plan to work toward and focus on the end goal. Why is it so complicated and why do we need a business plan?

A business plan is really something that, once you think it through and give lots of thought and understanding and research to your business, it becomes an *implementation* plan that you can put into action. It clarifies who your target customer is, where your target market is, how much you will need to spend when marketing your business, and who needs to know about you. A solid business plan allows you to intentionally run your business instead of your business running you.

Let's say you don't create a business plan. You start super excited, so your feet are off and running the moment you get your real estate license. You begin by taking some floor time in the office and holding open houses for other agents. There's nothing wrong with these activities, but here is what can eventually happen.

You get a lead. This person is interested in purchasing a house as a first-time homebuyer. The reason you typically start with a first-time homebuyer is because all of the other more experienced buyers have already worked with an agent in the past and, if that agent did a good job and kept in touch with them, they already have a working relationship. So, you get the leftovers.

These are also typically homes in a lower price range and need some work because the first-time buyer has no idea what they are doing (or what they should not be doing) during the transaction.

After showing this person 100 potential homes, they finally decide to make an offer on one. You get them under contract and have successfully scheduled a closing. It's the hardest money you've probably ever had to work for in your life.

The buyers, however, love you and appreciate all of the time you put in to help them. They gush about how wonderful their experience was and that you were such huge help in the purchase of their home. They go and tell all their friends. Then guess what happens. Their friends also want to become first-time homebuyers, so they call you. And so the cycle begins.

Don't get me wrong. There is a *ton* of satisfaction in helping first-time homebuyers, and there are some agents who want to focus their entire careers on helping this type of buyer. But it might not be what *you* envisioned *your* business to look like. The problem is that you may have never sat down and actually wrote out your vision. Researched it. Had clarity to it.

Maybe you envisioned selling luxury properties or repeat transactions to investors. Unfortunately, because you did not have a plan in place, you had nothing to put into action to make that vision a reality. That's what makes a business plan so powerful.

I've done more business plans in my life than I care to remember. However, I didn't open a majority of those businesses. Why? Because of the plan. Maybe there wasn't enough market share or there wasn't a need for the particular product I had in mind.

After all of my research and time dedicated, it turned out the business might not succeed after all. But do you know what? I'm okay with that because I'd rather spend 20 hours on a business plan that ultimately saved me over $100,000 than starting a business that wouldn't succeed anyway. These business plans have saved me hundreds of thousands of dollars over the course of my lifetime, and I'm not the only one.

Yes, it seems time consuming. You just want to get in, get started, and begin earning some money. But a little planning upfront can save you a ton of frustration and expense in the end. It can also put you on the path to success by providing extreme clarity.

It is *so* worth the time and effort and energy upfront to plan out your future. When you do this, your future plans for you. It aligns your career in such a way that you are able to achieve your goals more easily. All because you took the time to develop a step-by-step plan.

Accountability

Real estate is an exciting career. It gives us flexibility over our time and allows us to be our own boss. No more punching a time clock!

The downside to this line of thinking is, if we are not accountable for our actions and how we spend our time, this time might just slip away from us. We lose productivity. Losing productivity means losing transactions and losing transactions means losing revenue. In the long run, it means you'll go broke!

You've already set your goals. And if you've used the SMART method, you know how many transactions you need to sell this year to make that goal happen. You also know which educational courses you need to take within the next 12 months to give you a leg up over your competitors.

Who is going to guarantee that you get all of this done? Will your broker call you every morning, asking when you're going to arrive at the office? Probably not, I'm guessing.

In your real estate career, there is only one person who is accountable for what you do with your time—and who decides whether you will spend that time wisely—and that person is YOU!

At the end of the year, if you have not met your goals or accomplished your idea of success, then you have failed yourself. You may have also failed your family and your loved ones who are counting on you, but you have definitely failed yourself!

Accountability is basically defined as being responsible. I'm sure you consider yourself a responsible adult but are you? Who holds you accountable?

There are a few things we can do to increase our self-accountability. The first is to set goals. These can be long-term goals, such as 5 or 10 or 20-year goals, or they can be short-term goals, as in one year or less.

In addition to setting goals, we need to create a to-do list. Put this list in writing so it can keep you on track. Let it remind you what you have to get done so you keep moving forward in your business. I am a *huge* fan of a written to-do list and find that, when I lax off and quit keeping this written list, I start slipping with getting things accomplished.

A great recommended read for your to-do list and getting things accomplished overall is *Eat That Frog* by Brian Tracy. This is definitely on the recommended reading list on my website at www.CynthiaDeLuca.com and it's also on the top! Once you've read this book, you'll understand what I mean.

Another way to hold yourself accountable is to make appointments with your time. Throughout the course of the day (and the week), set a schedule with specific requirements of what you need to do with your time.

Maintaining your appointments and scheduling your actions is vital to success and accomplishing your goals. This topic is so important, we will discuss it more in the next chapter.

Your Previous Career

When focusing on you to help you have a more successful real estate career, it also helps to look at your current or previous career. Identify the skills you've learned and the qualities you've honed that can make you a better agent.

For example, if you have experience working as a nurse, you have likely honed your ability to really listen to people. To empathize with them and understand where they are at this point in time. You can use this skill as a real estate agent to get a better idea of the type of property your client wants or needs. This reduces the amount of time you will spend showing them homes that don't fit their specific situation.

Or maybe you've previously worked as a financial planner. This is a great skill to have as a real estate agent because you know how to create and stick to a reasonable budget, enabling you to make decisions that positively affect your bottom line. This skill also puts you in a good position to help your clients do the same.

Holding past positions in customer service, retail, or sales can also make you a better real estate agent. It improves your ability to develop a strong working relationship with your clients, taking what you've learned about how to make your customers feel valued so they continue to choose you as their service provider.

Take a moment right now and write down all of the jobs you've held in your life. For each one, list two or three skills you learned that can help you as you enter the world of real estate.

Jobs & Skills Learned:

____

____

____

____

____

____

____

____

____

____

____

Keep these skills in mind as you move forward in your career. Use them to help you achieve higher levels of success as these are your strengths and you will get further ahead the faster you learn to play off of them.

Other Streams of Income

Before we move on to the next chapter, I also want you to think about the streams of income you have available to you. This helps keep you and your family afloat financially as you begin to navigate your way through the real estate world.

If you are married or living with a partner, they may have a level of income that gives you some breathing room until you are able to start bringing in some serious money. This can help take the stress off as you begin your new venture.

If you don't have a partner who financially contributes to your household or you live alone, it can be beneficial to set up multiple streams of income to help support you in the beginning. This may include getting a part-time job, even if it isn't directly tied to real estate.

Once you get more established, you can develop more revenue streams by creating products for others. For example, I have written two books designed specifically for women who want to build wealth by buying rentals. They are *The High Heels Landlord: A Step-by-Step Guide for Women to Successful Real Estate Investing* and *Fill'Er Up: The High Heels Landlord's Guide to Filling Your Rental Property*.

Of course, that means I own rental properties, which all came after I started my real estate career. Those rentals offer me other streams of income.

I also offer a variety of video courses and worksheets at www.CynthiaDeLuca.com/shop that are helpful for those who want to enter this field but need a little help. These include:

- Buyer Questions for Leads
- Open House Feedback Form
- How to Prepare for a Showing in 10 Minutes or Less
- Transaction Timeline Checklist

Although all of these forms are free, I also offer a variety of documents at a cost to help others succeed in this field while also supplementing my income in real estate. For instance, I sell a Cash Flow Worksheet, an Office Policy Manual, and a Vacation Rental Manager Procedures document.

For those who take their transition into real estate seriously and want to learn how to reach success more quickly, I also provide several different courses (www.CynthiaDeLuca.com/courses-offered).

I also offer one-on-one private coaching sessions.

The point is, the more streams of income you create, the more stable you are financially. The more stable you are financially, the greater your level of freedom to do what you love.

Think about the things you can do to create multiple streams of income for you and your family. Identify your options relating to real estate, as well as any streams that interest you but aren't necessarily related to buying and selling properties. Create a SMART goal to get one or two of these in place.

Chapter Recap

- In real estate, you are your own company: *You, Inc.*
- When developing *You, Inc.*, consider how much time and money you can invest to build and grow your business.
- Determine your why and use this to help you continue to push forward on rough days.
- Set long-term goals and work your way backward, making sure they are SMART
- Always be involved in some type of professional development to stay current and relevant.

Continued….

- Develop a business plan so you know what you want (and don't want) in your real estate career.
- Create a system of personal accountability so you keep taking the actions that will make you a success.
- Consider the skills you've gained in your previous careers and how you can use them to become a top-notch real estate agent.
- Come up with at least one or two additional streams of income that can help support you financially as you start your real estate business, to take some of the pressure off.

Chapter 2

It's Really NOT About You

"I have been up against tough competition all my life. I wouldn't know how to get along without it."
Walt Disney

Embrace Competition

Have you ever heard the saying "What doesn't kill you makes you stronger"? That is how I view competition.

Think of how boring life would be if there was only one athlete to watch run a race at the Olympics. Or what if there was only one race car in the Daytona 500? No one would watch that.

"*As iron sharpens iron, so one person sharpens another*," Proverbs 27:17. What this means is that our competition makes us better. It makes us stronger.

Look around you in the real estate industry. Do we have a lot of competition? Of course, we do. There are hundreds of thousands of real estate professionals around us. So, yes, we have a ton of competition.

The interesting thing about our industry is that our competition is fully viewable. There are no secrets. In other words, if I want to find out how many transactions you sold last year, I can look it up in the Multiple Listing Service® (MLS). Not many other industries have this level of transparency available. So, checking out competition is an easy thing for us to do.

The other interesting thing about the real estate industry is that we're not just in competition with each other. We are also co-workers. Yep, you heard me right. Through the co-broke process, I want you to show my listing and I want to be able to show your listing. We need each other. In more ways than one.

Imagine you go on an appointment to get a new listing. The seller comments that he is also interviewing two other agents. In the end, he chooses one of these other real estate professionals.

You can either choose to drown in your own misery and rejection, or you can start doing a lot of research about your competition. Why did the seller choose them? What do they offer that is different from you? We put so much information out on our website and in our social media feeds that it's really easy to answer these questions just by doing a few quick searches.

No, I'm not a big fan of copying what your competition is doing. But don't you think that Lowes knows exactly what's going on at Home Depot and vice versa? You need to have a good grasp of your competition and what they offer. This enables you to better determine what you offer for your customers and how it is different from what your competition offers. It also helps you understand what you don't offer, can't offer, or don't want to offer.

Competition is everywhere and in every single industry. Once you know and understand the competition that surrounds you, you can up your game.

So, before you can get to work on improving yourself and what you offer, you need to embrace the competition. Understand the value it offers so you view it positively for what it is.

Play Hard to Get

I know it sounds crazy to talk about playing hard to get when we're talking about real estate but let me explain.

Let's say that recently when traveling to a new town, you were looking for a place to eat dinner. You look up an area that has a lot of restaurants nearby and choose one to visit. Upon arriving at that restaurant, you learn that there is a waiting list 45 minutes long.

During your wait, you look at the restaurant next door and see that it is totally empty. There's no one inside. Which one do you think has better service and better food?

We will almost always choose to wait in long lines for food or service we perceive as being better than to go to an empty restaurant that scares us because no one is eating there. I call this the *restaurant mentality*.

Think Starbucks or Chick-fil-A. You wait in long lines because you know that's the place to be. You don't mind waiting for the experience and the food that you want. Playing hard to get in real estate works in a similar manner.

Let's say your schedule is wide open. You have absolutely nothing going on – no listings and no buyers. A potential buyer calls and asks a few questions about one of your company's listings. You think you've talked to them enough to convince them to meet with you, so you ask them if they would like to see some houses. You say that your schedule is pretty free, so they can pick a date and time that's convenient for them.

Now let's look at a similar scenario that is handled a little differently. In this case, you still have a wide-open schedule, with no listings and no buyers. The potential buyer contacts you and is interested in a few properties and you want to show them these houses. You tell them you have only two available time slots left for the week and explain what dates and times those are. *Think restaurant mentality.*

People want to work with someone that they know is successful. When you are busy, also known as hard to get, they tend to work around your schedule for when you are available. They know that you must be someone who is sought after, and they want to work with you.

Conversely, if you tell your potential buyers that your schedule is wide open, so they can pick and choose the date, it's like an empty restaurant. They become scared of you, wondering why no one wants to work with you as a real estate agent. Eliminate this issue by doing things that make you seem hard to get.

Be Easy

Now I know this seems like a total contradiction since I just told you to play hard to get. However, I'm talking about something totally different than your schedule now.

When you think about the real estate process, regardless of how much you know or how confident you are because you've sold 100 properties, it is still very scary for buyers and sellers. The real estate transaction is an extremely complicated process that overwhelms many.

We know it as real estate agents because we do this day in and day out. We deal with frustrations like appraisal issues and inspection flaws and other issues fairly often. But to a buyer or a seller, this is a crisis that they encounter only once every 7 to 10 years, maybe longer.

In everything you do, try to be *easy*. Do your best to make the process simple to understand and easy to get through.

Think about the iPhone when it first was released in 2007. It had massive success in the first two years. Millions were sold and it totally changed the way we think about these phones that we carry around in our pockets.

If you own one, think about when you opened the box to your very first iPhone. Did it come with a 400-page instruction manual? No. Is it a complicated device? Yes, it can do many things.

Despite this, it is so easy to use that we can pick it up and begin to make calls or surf the internet almost immediately. Even people who aren't tech-savvy don't have to go through hours and hours of training to learn how to use its functions. This device is complicated, but it's also easy.

Think about the stress and frustration that you can take away from your customers and strive to do this at all times. That is really what your job is. It is finding ways to make the process of buying or selling property easier for them to understand and engage in.

Think about this the next time you go through a real estate transaction. In every single facet of the process, from completing all the necessary paperwork to making phone calls to everything else. Always ask yourself this question: Is there a way to make it easier?

If you are unsure what you can do to make real estate transactions easier for your clients, talk to the ones you've worked with in the past. Ask them what areas were the most difficult to understand. Inquire what you could have done to lessen some of those difficulties.

If you're new to real estate, look up online reviews for other real estate agents in your area. Happy customers will write reviews explaining what they enjoyed about the process, what the agent did to make it easier to get through. Unhappy clients will share the areas they felt were most complex and challenging.

Both types of reviews give you insight into the buyers' and sellers' minds. They also give you an idea of what you can do to differentiate yourself from your competition. They tell you which processes you need to simplify to get the best results.

Think also about the topics or processes that you found the most confusing when you first began to learn them. If you had a hard time understanding these things, it's likely that some of your clients will feel the same way. Figure out how to help them overcome this confusion. Find a way to be easy.

What's the Worst They Can Say?

Rejection is something that no one appreciates. We take it personally. We take it to heart. In a career that involves any type of sales, you will inevitably be rejected many, many times. If you let it, this can create self-doubt and cause you to give up on your dreams.

I want you to start thinking about rejection a little bit differently. First, let me pose this question to you: What's the worst thing your clients can say to you? The answer to this question is "no." This is the absolute worst thing a buyer or seller can say to you. So, what do you have to lose?

The first week I started my career my sales manager told me to drive around the area, find for sale by owner signs, and then call them. He gave me some scripts to read to the FSBO seller and wished me luck. Being the obedient person I am, I did exactly what he said. I drove around, found my first FSBO, and called. When a woman answered the phone, I started reading from my script. It was something like why she should hire a professional because we can go show the house anytime and it may not be convenient for the seller. She politely but sternly informed me that she lived right next door and could show the house anytime someone wanted to see it and she didn't need a real estate professional. She also informed me that she knew every big real estate broker in town and didn't need an agent, she personally knew plenty of them to choose from. That was my first no.

According to the scripts, it suggested calling once a week, so I decided to call her the following week and read script 2. Besides, I had nothing else to do, so why not. The second script was something like how a real estate professional can host an open house for you and gain buyers through that process. She mentioned she was already planning on having an open house that weekend and she didn't need me. That was my second no.

When I called her the third week, literally reading line by line my script, I said something like "I'm sorry to hear you didn't have a good turnout for your open house". That's when she stopped me and explained she had over 50 people visit her open house. Wow! That was my third no.

I called her on week 4 and, according to the script, might have potential buyers looking and I'd love to come to see the house so I know if it will match any of their needs. Funny thing is, I had no buyers. Not a one…So she tells me to stop by and preview the house. As we are walking through the house, it was awful. It was a historical house, unlivable with absolutely nothing going for it except the original clawfoot bathtub upstairs. We arrive back at the front door, script in hand, and I start reading directly from it, right in front of her! The script basically was asking if I could list the property, then it would expose the property to not just my buyers, but many more. She politely opened the door and escorted me out. She was not at all interested. That was my fourth no.

The fifth week, I called her and started reading the script. I had barely started when she interrupted me and said "It's obvious you're not going to leave me alone until I list my house with you, so if you can be here within 15 minutes, I'll give you the listing." And that is how I got my first listing.

Even if you ask someone if they need a real estate agent and they say no, it doesn't necessarily mean no. It simply means "not right now." If you've ever studied a sales funnel, then you already know that you have to put a lot of numbers and opportunities into the top. If you do this, eventually a sale will come out of the bottom.

Take a look at the sales funnel on the next page.

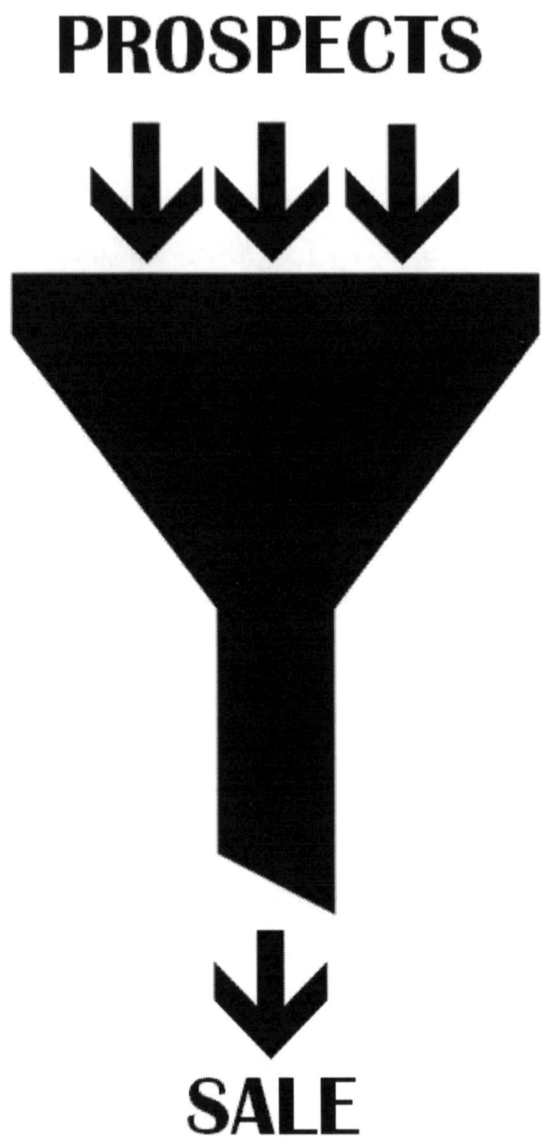
PROSPECTS
SALE

Now let's imagine that you're at the top of your sales funnel except, this time, you're asking your buyers and sellers a lot of questions. Yes, a lot of them are going to say no. But the more you ask, eventually you will get to a yes which will come out of the bottom of the funnel and result in a sale.

Every time you hear the word no, you're one step closer to a yes.

When you hear a no, think about it joyfully and with excitement. Let it be a trigger, a nudge to remind you that you've got to keep moving until you get to a yes, and you're one step closer!

For example, if you track your stats and determine that you have to ask 100 people if they need a real estate agent before someone says yes, when you hear the first no, you now only have 99 more to go. When you hear the second no, now you're at 98, and so on.

For a wonderful story on applying this, I recommend reading *Go For No, Yes is the Destination* by Richard Fenton. (Again, a link can be found on my website at www.CynthiaDeLuca.com, along with links to all of the other readings I recommend.)

By the way, the seller from my first listing went on to use me for 4 more transactions over the next few years and referred me on several other transactions. She became very loyal to me, and I got to know her and her family well. Some years later, she passed away fairly unexpectedly. My brother and sister-in-law adopted her twin boys, age 11 at the time, and now they are my nephews. I am reminded every day that when you hear the word no, you must ignore it, because it literally can alter the course of your life!

Be a Problem Solver

Imagine that you're a listing agent and you get a phone call from a buyer's agent letting you know that a particular property did not appraise at the sales price. We now have a problem.

You might be quick to pick up the phone, contact your seller, and let them know what's going on. We want to keep them involved right? We want to make sure they know what's going on and that we're working for them behind the scenes.

But if we call them and tell them that the property has not appraised, they might ask us a follow-up question: *What now?* The seller is going to want to know what comes next.

If you have not taken the time to explore any of the possible solutions, then all you've done is dump a problem in their lap. Make that phone call at 5:30 in the evening, and now you've robbed them of their sleep tonight *and* created more worry.

Commit right now to never, ever call your seller or buyer (or anyone else for that matter) with a problem. Instead, always call them with a *solution.* Give them the opportunity to make a decision that will allow them to move forward toward your ultimate goal of the transaction closing.

Back to the original scenario where the buyer's agent calls you to notify you that the appraised value came in less than the sales price and the lender will not allow the transaction to move forward until you figure it out. The first question I'd ask is if the buyer is willing to pay more for the property. If the answer is no, then I'd ask him to meet halfway. If the answer is still no, that's when I look at my other options.

At this point, one solution may be for the seller to consider lowering their sales price to meet the appraised value. Or they may decide to cancel this contract, put the property back on the market, and find a new buyer to get a new appraisal.

Another option might be a second appraisal. Of course, only if the lender allows it and if they find fault with the first appraisal. But it's worth asking.

Now that I've determined all of the possibilities (and what is *not* a possibility), I can then contact my seller. This may be a day or two later, but again, if I have nothing to offer the seller but the problem, I'm not solving anything.

I'm going to wait until I have a list of all available options before I contact the seller and explain that the property did not appraise for the sales price. This is also when I say that I've already checked to see if we can do option A, option B, or option C. Now the seller gets to decide between these three and figures out how to move forward in their lives, and with the transaction. I am not putting them in a situation where they are going to be sitting around worrying about what's next, worrying about the unknown.

Commit to always being a problem solver. Not a problem creator or someone who is known for dumping problems on someone else's lap. Earn a reputation as someone who is willing to put in the work necessary to give their clients an option when things don't go exactly as planned.

I've had problems with survey encroachments, title defects, lack of probate, property defects, termites, and everything in between. And in these situations, I'm always searching for the solution that will get us to the next step. The one that will move us toward a transaction closing.

Any time a problem arises in any transaction, my first question is, "How can we fix this?" There is almost always a solution if the parties are willing to do the work and put forth the effort.

Do not focus on the problem or you will never get anywhere. Always focus on what the possible options are to fix the problem. Strive to create solutions. If your buyer and seller are willing to work at it, you can make the problem go away and move forward in the transaction.

Service

We sell houses, right? Well, sort of. I believe that what we really sell is our service.

When you think about a buyer or seller hiring an agent to help them through a real estate transaction, there is lots of competition that they can choose from to help them. A lot of us might be members of the same multiple listing service, we have the same options available for marketing and advertising, and a lot of the things that we offer might be remarkably similar. So, what sets us apart and why do buyers and sellers hire us instead?

I believe a big part of why they hire us is our service. So let me ask you, what type of customer service experience are you offering?

Think about some of the places you patronize and why you do business there. For example, I do business with Publix supermarkets, Chick-fil-A, Disney World, Zappos shoes, and the Ritz Carlton because of the service I get at these locations.

There are lots of places that I could go grocery shopping, but I choose Publix because it truly is where shopping is a pleasure (which happens to their slogan). The customer service they exude is absolutely 100% intentional. They do not just tell you which aisle the sugar is on, but they walk you to the aisle and show you the exact spot where the product is. That is something that you don't get at other grocery stores in my area.

And who would've thought that a fast-food restaurant would pay someone to walk around their dining room and offer to refill drinks, which actually costs the company more money? Who would have thought they would also give you a mint and a wet wipe while telling you it was their pleasure to serve you? Chick-fil-A has shown us that a fast-food restaurant can greatly improve their customer service and they will have lifelong customers as a result.

Then there's Walt Disney's dream of Disney World. The whole experience takes you into another world of reality. A world where you forget who you are, and your entire life, even if just for the day as they sprinkle you with pixie dust and whisk you off your feet. You are completely surrounded by an enormous cast of customer service cast members. It truly is a memorable experience.

What makes all of these companies so unique with what they offer? They've made customer service an intentional practice. They've made a conscious decision about what they will offer and how they will go—which is above and beyond—for what I call *wow* moments.

These *wow* moments are unexpected moments that surpass anyone's expectations. Moments that truly surprise you due to the intensely high level of customer service.

Think about the places you shop or the restaurants you eat at. What type of customer service do you get that keeps you going back?

Think also about what *you* offer as a customer service experience to your customers. Is it just the normal, typical experience or do you *wow* them with anything? Be honest when answering this question. If you are not doing anything right now to go above and beyond, you can easily change this.

What are some ways that you could provide your customers with a *wow* experience?

- Packing snacks when going to view properties with buyers
- Packing a small cooler of ice water in the trunk for hot days out with buyers
- Carrying a small broom and dustpan and some Febreeze with you to stop by your listing before the showing to give it a fresh smell and quick sweep by the front door

There are so many ways you can *wow* your customers. You just need to look for the opportunities. Think about what it is you offer, how you offer it, and how you can up your game for your next customer.

Who Is Your Target Customer?

Let's be real for a second. You have to be somewhat good at sales or else you'll never convince a buyer or seller to use you as their agent.

That said, making a sale is less about your skills and more about your target customer. What do I mean by this?

Imagine that you sell vacuum cleaners door to door. When you get to the first door of the day, a young man answers. You spend the next 15-20 minutes telling him how wonderful the vacuum works, all of the great features it has, and how you offer several pricing options, so it is affordable on any budget. You've even amazed yourself with your sales pitch, yet he tells you no and closes the door.

When you arrive at the next house, before you can even begin your sales pitch, the homeowner says, "A new vacuum? That's great! My current one is so difficult to push that I hardly ever use it!"

Unbeknownst to the person answering the door, they just gave you enough information to help you make your sale. They've told you a *pain point* that they have with their current vacuum, offering you the opportunity to show exactly how yours excels in this area.

If you don't know what your potential customers like and dislike, it is incredibly difficult to make a sale. You must thoroughly understand what brings them pain and what brings them pleasure so you can hit both of these points with your services.

This is why many successful salespersons spend more time *asking* questions and allowing their potential buyers to talk. The more information these people share, the easier it is to identify which products and features would appeal to them most.

In real estate, how do you determine your target market? Think about the type of person you enjoy working with most. Is it the first-time homebuyer who is looking for the perfect starter home? Or would you prefer to work with someone who buys and sells property regularly, like an investor, and is just looking for an agent to assist with the transaction?

Once you identify your target customer, seek to learn as much about them as you can. Do they like to eat out a lot? If so, what restaurants do they frequent? A gift certificate to one of these establishments upon closing is a great way to thank them for doing business with you.

Or maybe you learn that your target customer often has children. Keeping a few toys in your vehicle can help keep the little ones busy while you're showing a property, which the parents will appreciate.

Also, seek to identify what keeps your target market up at night. What bothers them the most? What are some of the worries that many of them have in common?

The more you understand how your target audience thinks, what they do, what they won't do, what they prefer, what they avoid, and so on, the more you can tailor your service offerings and marketing efforts in a more appealing way.

Some of this information you can collect while working with your target customer. Strike up a normal conversation and ask what type of music they like, what type of food they prefer to eat, how far they went in school, and what career they are in. Over time, you will begin to see patterns emerge. This will give you a better idea of who your market is.

Another way to better understand the people you want to work with most is to look at their social media. Pay attention to the things they share, the posts they comment on, and which ones they like. You can learn a lot about someone just based on their social media pages.

If you have a good list of clients already, send out a questionnaire to learn more about them. To entice them to answer and send it back, make it anonymous. This prevents them from not responding out of fear that they'll share too much private information.

Again, you're not just looking for what they like and dislike when it comes to real estate. Yes, this type of information will help you do your job. But the more you know about them as a whole, the easier it is to develop a marketing strategy that resonates with them. And the easier it is to close a sale.

Let me give you some examples. Next time you have the TV on, and a commercial starts for a retirement investor, pay attention to the music. They might be playing something like a Billy Joel song or The Beach Boys. Why? Because it resonates with their customer. They know who their customer is and they are talking their language, sort of speak.

Another might be the next commercial you see for reverse mortgages. Pay attention to the spokesperson. Maybe it's Tom Selleck or the late Fred Thompson. Think of their age and who their target customer is? You won't see the Kardashian's playing in this role, that's not their target customer.

Starving for 7 Years

When I was early on in my real estate career, I had a friend ask me what I was going to do while I starved for seven years. Not understanding what he meant by this, I asked for clarification. "Starving for seven years? What do you mean?"

My friend explained that, at that time, the national average of how long it took a seller to sell their house, move, and relocate was once every seven years. He explained that if I had to wait seven years for my current buyer to become a repeat customer, I would starve in between. That point hit home.

I couldn't wait seven years for a repeat customer. Can you imagine? What in the world what I do for the next seven years? I had to go find new customers constantly, over and over and over again, because I could not wait years for repeat customers.

After several nights of losing sleep, I went back to this person and asked him what he recommended. He was an insurance salesman, so he explained how he got paid every year when someone renewed their insurance. He continued the relationship with his customers, getting more income year after year.

I started soul-searching, asking myself what I could do to get repeat business sooner than once every seven years. What other options were there to find business? How could I make this process quicker? From that soul-searching, I determined a few things.

One is that I decided my target customer would not be a buyer or seller, but someone who could give me the business of plenty of buyers and sellers. Secondly, I had to figure out exactly who this person was.

I came up with an entire list of possibilities. It could be a CPA, a financial advisor, an insurance agent, a home inspector, or pretty much any of our vendors that regularly come in contact with people looking for real estate.

It could be a divorce attorney who knows people getting divorced and needing to sell their house. It could be an estate attorney who needs to sell the house for the deceased's heirs.

Also on my list were influential people. These were people that know a lot of people that can continue to give you more and more and more business. We will discuss this more in Section 2.

After I compiled my list of places and categories where I could get repeat business over and over, I went back and looked at the list to determine what I thought my likelihood was of connecting with people in my community in these categories. I decided that the CPA and financial advisor weren't necessarily the thing for me. But I *was* very interested in the estate planner.

I live in Florida and we have a lot of people who retire here and eventually die, so the opportunity for that type of real estate is endless. In fact, some people refer to Florida as the frog state…where people come to croak. I started looking in my area to see how many attorneys there were that handle these types of cases and figuring out how I could connect with them. Then I made the decision that, before I could do any of these transactions, I had to learn the probate process inside and out.

I want to be very clear with you. This is *not* for everyone and this may not be the path that you decide is your way out of starvation. But for me, it was a good fit. After starting some research, I quickly realized how interesting this all was and even contemplated going to law school. I really like reading law, so I found my niche. (More on niches in a little bit).

The upside when it comes to probate and death is that nobody ever knows when it's going to happen. But it is definite that it *is* going to happen, eventually. So, after I determined this was the way for me, I started researching how many people in my area were dying and on what type of consistent level. That's when I hit the goldmine.

No more starving for seven years waiting on a repeat customer. The attorney would become my client and refer me to *their* clients, who had the need to sell, and I was in! Repeat business galore.

I just had to figure out how to get in the door with the probate attorneys. Again, I'm going to make you wait until a future chapter, in the niche section, to learn how I did it. But in the meantime, what's *your* plan?

Currently, the starvation rate is about every 12 years according to the National Association of REALTORS® Home Buyer and Seller survey. Do you really want to wait 12 years before your customer decides they need you again? No? Then what other resources exist around you that could be sending you repeat business on a constant basis?

Maybe it's builders when they have buyers coming in to build a new house and they need to list and sell their old house. The options are endless. Just look for the opportunities and take action once you recognize them.

The Value You Bring

When building your customer base, it's important to recognize that the more value you bring, the more inclined buyers and sellers will be to hire you.

Obviously, part of your value is the knowledge of how to navigate the real estate transaction process. But every agent offers this same ability. So, what kind of additional value can you bring to the table to draw more customers in?

To answer this question, put yourself in the shoes of your buyers. What can you do to stand out from every other agent in the field?

For example, if you tend to work with homebuyers who are moving in from another state, you could create a cheat sheet of the local utility companies and their contact information. This makes their move so much easier because they know exactly which companies to contact.

People moving long distances would also benefit from having a checklist of all the things they need to do to make their transition more successful. Include items such as canceling auto-pay on all of their old utility companies so they don't have money withdrawn from their accounts while they are closing them and reminding them to transfer their vehicle's plates to the new state within the allotted time.

Another option is to create a private Facebook group for all of your customers. This gives people who are new to the area a group they can go to if they want recommendations about where to eat, who is the best mechanic, or which company offers the most affordable home repairs. Plus it helps them meet new friends.

You can also increase your value by raising your level of customer service. This could include working with mortgage companies that will go to your customer's new home to finalize the closing. It might also involve sending your buyers and sellers an email every couple of days to provide an updated status on the process.

The more value you can provide, the more you will be a sought-after real estate professional. When people know that working with you means that they will enjoy a few extras, you quickly become the only agent they want to do business with.

Not sure how to increase your value? Ask potential buyers and sellers what you can do to help make their move go more smoothly. Even if they say that there is nothing, the fact that you offered will go a long way.

Chapter Recap

- Embrace your competition because they are the ones who will make you better and stronger.

Continued….

- Play hard to get so your customers see you as a busy professional, one they are willing to wait for, think *restaurant mentality*.
- Strive to make the real estate transaction as easy as possible for your customers.
- Remember that the worst thing your customers can say is "no," which isn't all that bad; plus, every no gets you one step closer to a yes!
- Earn a reputation as a problem solver, giving your customers solutions versus frustration and worry.
- Customers hire you for the service you offer, so do what it takes to provide the best.
- Know your target customer inside and out as this will tell you how to market your services in a way that truly resonates with (and captivates) them.
- Instead of starving for years, seek to discover resources that will provide a continual river of customers.
- Come up with ways to elevate the value you bring to the table and you will become a sought-after real estate professional.

Chapter 3
Developing You

"Growth is the great separator between those who succeed and those who do not."
John C. Maxwell, Leadership Coach and Bestselling Author

Get a Mentor

One of the fastest ways to get where you want to be—whether personally or professionally—is to find someone who is already there and learn from them. Make them your mentor. Use their experiences to help you reach higher peaks while also avoiding some of their pitfalls along the way.

Getting a mentor is like getting a coach. This is someone who is intimately familiar with the game and knows all the tips and tools needed to help you get a win.

In real estate, a good mentor to pursue is someone who is in the area of real estate you desire. For instance, if you want to work primarily with individuals interested in buying or selling apartment buildings, find an agent who has this type of clientele. If your passion is helping young couples purchase their first home, work with a successful agent who does the same.

The person you choose must be someone who not only works in your desired field but has also mastered it. Don't just assume that they're doing well, look at their sales records. Are they closing a lot of deals? If not, you're more likely to pick up bad habits versus good.

It's also important to select someone who is willing to be your mentor. Not everyone has the time or desire to take on an apprentice of sorts. They'd rather just do what they do and go home at the end of the day.

One way to initiate the mentor-mentee relationship is to connect with them on social media. Like their business page on Facebook or ask them to connect on LinkedIn. Like and comment on their posts to show that you are interested in what they have to say.

If you know someone who already has a pre-established relationship with the person you'd like to be your mentor, ask them to make an introduction. This could be at a local networking event or even via email. Having this other person vouch for you goes a long way in being welcomed by your desired mentor.

Once the connection has been made, whether by you directly or someone you know, it may be tempting to jump right in and ask them to teach you everything they know. However, taking this approach will almost always ensure that they will say no.

Instead, court this new relationship the same way you would if getting to know someone that you're interested in personally. Take it slow and give them a chance to get to know you. Help them realize that you are a good person, that you are someone who respects their knowledge and time. The more they get to know, like, and trust you, the easier it will be for them to agree to be your mentor.

Also, don't make your new professional relationship all about you. You must both benefit from the connection or it isn't going to work. Offer to help them out with a project or donate your time at one of their open houses. If you appear to be in it for only your benefit, they will be less likely to give you their free time.

After you've established some level of trust, offer to take them out to lunch. This gives you the opportunity to learn their story, strengthening your connection even more. It also enables you to ask how they've succeeded in real estate. Ask if they're willing to share their best pieces of advice to someone new in the field.

Some agents will gladly give you an hour or two of their time, especially if you are appreciative and not overly assertive. Others have the heart of a teacher and will willingly give more. Seek to identify their level of willingness upfront so you don't overstep your bounds or overstay your welcome.

Along the same lines, once you've become a successful agent yourself, help new agents in the field by agreeing to mentor them. Pass on the great information you've learned from *your* mentors to help them increase their success. Give them the same time and respect that previous mentors have given to you.

What do you do if you can't find a local real estate agent who is interested in stepping in the role of a mentor? You may find yourself in this position if you tend to be shy and have a hard time reaching out to someone you don't know. This may also be an issue if you work in a rural area and there aren't many agents around.

Either way, if you don't have access to a physical person to use as a mentor, seek to learn from some of the greatest real estate agents of all time. Read their books to get a better idea of the strategies that worked best for them, as well as those that didn't.

Among my recommended readings for real estate specifically are *21 Things I Wish My Broker Had Told Me* by Frank Cook and *The Millionaire Real Estate Agent* by Gary Keller. Both of these books are full of great advice for agents who desire higher levels of success. (You can find more recommended reads at www.CynthiaDeLuca.com/recommended-reading.)

Becoming a Team

Teams are growing in popularity in the real estate industry. A team is when two or more agents decide to work together full-time with all their transactions. There are some pros and cons to joining or developing a team. Let's go over some of the basics here.

One of the pros of being part of a team is that there are two (or more) of you to handle all the work. Maybe one of you focuses primarily on paperwork while the other spends the majority of their time one-on-one with customers. Taking this type of approach enables you to get more done in less time since there are two of you to do the work versus one of you trying to do it all.

Working with a partner also makes it possible to focus on the parts of the job that align best with your individual strengths. If you are good with details, for instance, you may be the team member responsible for ensuring that all the contracts are complete. If your strength is that you are a people person, your talents would be better suited talking to potential clients, connecting with them in a way that makes them want to choose you as their real estate agent.

Teaming up with another agent is a great way to grow your business by bringing in a partner who specializes in areas outside of your normal realm. This shows potential customers that you have experience in a wide variety of real estate transactions. This can be more appealing to buyers and sellers who are interested in several areas of real estate as well.

Becoming part of a team also gives you access to the knowledge, tips, and tricks the other agent has learned in their real estate career. It gives you someone you can bounce ideas off if you are unsure how to proceed with a particular transaction or encounter a problem you can't figure out how to solve.

At a minimum, having a partner in your real estate venture can make the days seem not so long because you have someone to talk to, laugh with, and share your experiences. But there are cons to teams as well.

For instance, when you join forces with another real estate professional, your success is dependent on their success. If they don't pull their weight, they're going to drag you down and make it harder for you to achieve your goals.

Teaming up also means that you split your profits. So, if you score a sweet real estate deal that brings in a lot of cash, you have to share the landfall with your partner...maybe even if they weren't involved in the transaction at all.

Another disadvantage of teams is that, if it doesn't work out, it requires a fair deal of work to separate the partnership. In addition to needing new marketing that only lists one of your names, you may have to create an entirely new business. This eliminates any brand recognition you have worked hard to create.

If you do decide to take this route, choose your teammate carefully. Select someone who you not only mesh with professionally but also someone who you get along with personally. Since you will be spending a lot of time together, it is important that you get along.

Doing personality tests helps identify how well you will work together. Check your communication styles to make sure they mesh.

Additionally, be very clear about your expectations and who is responsible for what. Being detailed about each person's role reduces any misunderstanding after the fact. It also ensures that everyone involved knows exactly what is expected from them for the partnership to be successful.

Having a contract that outlines your agreement protects both parties involved. If you are in search of team agreements and procedures on how to operate your team, feel free to check out my website, www.CynthiaDeLuca.com, and look in the shop for the Team Procedures Manual and the Independent Contractor Agreement for a Team or Assistant.

Take the time to tend to all of these issues *before* you make the decision to enter into a team. This allows you to set clear expectations for both of you. It also gives you the opportunity to decide whether this is the right decision for you instead of jumping in without doing your homework and then realizing that you can't work together.

Defining Your Niche

You might've heard this term before, but what does it really mean to have a niche in real estate?

To be in a niche in a particular area of real estate means that you are an expert, or you have a substantial amount of knowledge in that area, whether through education or transactional experience. A niche is a way to focus on a particular type of property or to serve a specific demographic group.

One benefit of defining a niche is that you become a master in that particular area. For example, selling duplexes and triplexes is a different type of transaction than selling the average house. Without the necessary expertise, you might struggle through this kind of transaction. And because you are less than familiar with selling duplexes and triplexes, you could also provide your customer less-than-stellar advice.

Will the deal end with added liability? Will you get sued? Unfortunately, neither of these scenarios is off the table.

Now imagine the same scenario but, this time, you are a real estate agent who is an expert with these types of sales in your market area. This allows you to breeze through the transaction with fewer struggles and snags because you know exactly what to look for and exactly what to expect.

Plus, if you are known for your expertise in a specific area of real estate, other agents might prefer to hand you a buyer within your demographic and take a referral fee instead. This is especially true if it is a type of property that they know nothing or very little about. This is just one example of how having a niche can increase your value and, subsequently, raise your income level.

I was in my office one day catching up on some files when I received a phone call. Less then half a mile down the road was a competiting real estate company. On the phone was an agent from that office who asked if I would be willing to accept a referral and that the customers were currently in his office and he could send them down immediately. He carried on to say the buyers were looking for a duplex, and he had never sold an investment property before, but knew I had a lot of experience in that market and specialized in it because he saw it on my personal brochure. We agreed on a referral fee amount and within 30 minutes, the eager buyers were standing in my office.

Some real estate professionals say it is a scary thought to pick and advertise a niche because they feel like they will lose business. I have found the exact opposite to be true. Having a niche actually raises your level of transactions, business, and expertise in the marketplace. Wouldn't you rather work with a specialist than a generalist for your transaction?

For most people, the answer is yes. If you have a questionable mole, would you rather go to a doctor who is a generalist or one who specializes in skin issues? Going to the latter gives you a greater feeling of confidence because you know that this professional has the knowledge to identify whether the mole is precancerous or of no concern.

This is the type of professional you want to be for your real estate clients. You want them to know that, when they come to you for a particular transaction, you have the knowledge necessary to give them the best outcome possible. The only real question is whether you decide what your niche is or if you allow your niche to find you.

For instance, if you work with a lot of first-time homebuyers when beginning your real estate career, they will likely provide referrals to their network of friends, who are also in the market to buy their first home. As more people in this demographic are referred to you, by default, it becomes your niche. Your niche has found you.

The other option involves seeking to find your niche and being intentional about it. For example, you might decide to go learn everything you can about the probate process and selling real estate that is included in a deceased person's estate. From there, you go and promote yourself to the attorneys handling these types of transactions so that you become the premier real estate agent selling those properties.

In this example, you intentionally found your niche, the opposite of allowing your niche to find you. The first being considered a reaction, the second an intentional action, or a more proactive approach.

Do you want to be *reactive* or *proactive*?

Either way, you become known as the expert with regard to a particular type of property or demographic of a client, which means you have a niche. If you promote it and tell everyone you know about your niche, you will quickly become the expert for that type of sale.

One final clarification about your niche. Just because you choose a niche does not mean that you have to turn away every other type of business. You just need to be aware of how much of other types of business you take on.

Consider defining your niche today. Do you have a certain type of property transaction or location of sale that you have done a lot of? When going back and reviewing that, what are the majority of your transactions? Your niche may have already found you, even if you didn't realize it.

If your niche has not yet picked you, think about the areas of real estate that you enjoy most. If you are unsure, consider the areas you'd love most to learn about.

Maybe you currently offer services related to residential real estate, but you think you'd like to do commercial real estate instead. If you don't already know how to conduct this type of transaction, seek to learn it. Take classes to expand your knowledge so you can make this your niche.

Perhaps you work in an area where industrial business is alive and well. You could increase your knowledge of buying and selling buildings used for the production or storage of goods. If you live in a farming community, take classes about the buying and selling of vacant land.

Take the actions necessary to develop the expertise in these specific areas. That way, when someone wants to buy or sell this type of property, you will be the agent they think of going to first. You will be the specialist they seek to help them make the right decision for their financial health.

Chapter Recap

- Getting a mentor can help you achieve higher levels of success at a faster rate.
- There are pros and cons to creating a team, so enter this type of dynamic carefully.
- Define your niche now so you can become recognized for your expertise in a specific area of real estate.

Section 2

Bigwig Status

Chapter 4

Who Do You Know?

"Networking is an investment in your business. It takes time and, when done correctly, can yield great results for years to come."

Diane Helbig, Business & Leadership Development Advisor

Building Your Database (Who Should Know You?)

I believe that on day one of your career, every real estate agent should sit down and write a list of every single person they can think of in the local area and market that they work. Heck just scan your contacts in your cell phone to start. The next step is to let all those people know that you are now in real estate. This essentially becomes your database and sphere of influence.

In the future, you can add contacts created from closed transactions, open house guests, buyers, and really anyone you meet. This should be relatively easy because these individuals should already be in your CRM, or Customer Relationship Management database.

One of the beautiful things about an online CRM system is that you can place tags on customers' names. These are similar to what we know today as hashtags. Using tags makes your database more searchable, so it becomes easier to find past clients.

With an online CRM, you can go in and do a search to pull up just those people in your database under that specific tag. Or you can pull multiple categories at once, like a past client who is also a personal friend.

Tags enable you to have the same person entered into multiple databases without having to create a double or triple entry. When a current buyer becomes a past customer after the closing, just go into the CRM and change the tag to reflect their status change from buyer to previous customer. Some examples might be:

#PastCustomer
#CurrentBuyer
#OpenHouseGuest
#PersonalFriend

You can get detailed and tag in many ways. Or you can keep it simple. Something like:

#PastCustomer
#CurrentCustomer
#FutureCustomer

The #FutureCustomer is for anyone that you met at an open house, social event, etc. that you hope will someday use you.

Your database is the key to a long and successful career in real estate. If you build a quality database and keep in touch with that database, you won't have to advertise to the general public or work with strangers in the future of your career.

Think about that for a moment. You never have to work with a stranger again. Your database can actually give you *all* your customers, whether you've worked with them in the past or they are referrals from those you have in your database.

Your CRM is basically your Rolodex of people that you want to know that you are in real estate and that you hope to gain business from. You can find lots of different CRM systems specifically built for real estate.

Some are free and some cost money on an ongoing basis. Check with your brokerage company first as it might have something for everyone to utilize.

Otherwise, when choosing a CRM system, look for the export option. If the data is not yours, meaning you cannot download or extract it, it's time to find a different system.

I would also highly recommend that you make a list before selecting a particular CRM. This list should contain all of the items that you want and need the program to do for you.

There are lots of ways the system can automate certain practices for you. Of course, the more bells and whistles it has, the more it's going to cost.

When you're first starting in your career, you're probably just looking for a basic system to input your data and keep track of it. However, a CRM can do so much more for you. It can send out monthly e-newsletters, keep track of when you should be contacting your customers, and all kinds of automated functions to tell you what you need to do each day and who you need to contact.

Write your list of needs and wants and use it to look for a software system that meets them. There's no sense in paying for more bells and whistles than you'll ever need.

Have you ever heard the saying that your network equals your net worth? Increase your net worth by filling your database with everyone you know, followed by building a campaign to keep in touch. (We'll touch on this more later.)

Get Your Five a Day

You've heard the old saying that eating an apple a day will help you stay in good health. Well, I have a new saying for your business. *"Pass out five a day before you call it quits today."*

One of the quickest, easiest, and least expensive ways to get your name out and start business happening in 90 days or less is to pass out five business cards a day. This involves keeping them somewhere that is easily accessible. This could be your pants pocket or if you're a lady, a side pocket of your purse. Either way, these cards need to be somewhere that is easy to access so you're not digging in the bottom of your purse with all the crumbs, and who knows what else is down there.

Your goal at the end of each day is to pass out at least five business cards to people you do not already know. This means that at the end of each week containing five working days, you will have passed out 25 business cards to people who had no idea you exist!

Do this for a month and you will see the potential of how much exposure you are able to get. Remember the sales funnel? Think of how many more leads you are dropping into the top of that funnel, giving you more at the bottom as a result.

Passing out five a day means you cannot sit in the comfort of your office and wait for people to come to you. You must get out and about in your community and network. You must be in the same places where others go and share your business cards there.

One of the easiest places to pass out your five a day is the grocery store. Many people head to the supermarket between 4:30 and 6:00 every evening after work. It's packed with potential buyers and sellers. Come dressed for success and open for business with your name tag on and ready to meet new people. Here's how my grocery store farming works:

As soon as I enter the grocery store, I grab a shopping cart and head straight for the milk aisle. This also works with any other type of food product that you use on an ongoing basis. My son happens to drink almost a gallon of milk every day, therefore, I'm constantly buying it.

Once in the milk aisle, I grab a carton of milk and put it in my shopping cart. Then I proceed to slowly stroll up and down each aisle trying to make eye contact with every shopper that I can. If someone locks eyes with me then it's on. I'll smile, nod, and start the conversation with something like: "Wow! Can you believe the price of milk? I can't believe how expensive it is. At least real estate is still a good deal."

Yes, cheesy, I know. But it works because *everybody* wants to talk about real estate. They either own a home, want to sell a home, or they have the American dream of buying a home.

Still, sometimes they do look away. Other times they'll nod, shake their head yes, and then look away. The ones you're looking to meet are those who respond, opening the door to further conversation.

For example, they might respond with something like, "Yeah, the house across the street from me just sold and I can't believe the price they got for it" or "Yes, there was a house down the road from me that I was keeping an eye out to see how much it sold for."

It really doesn't matter what they say as long as they open up the door to further conversation. That's when I say, "Oh, by the way, here's my card." I don't put a ton of pressure on them and I don't give a whole long speech about if they ever want to buy or sell or refer anybody they've ever met in their life to me, please make sure they give me a call. I just hand them my card and tell them that if they ever need anything to let me know. Then I walk away.

This approach works like a charm! It's short, sweet, to the point, and piques their curiosity. If I don't find anybody to lock eyes with up and down each aisle, I stand in the longest checkout line possible and try to make eye contact with the person in front of or behind me. The conversation happens roughly the same way.

Many agents are told to "farm" a geographic area or neighborhood. I think this approach is awful, but if you farm the grocery store often, even the cashiers and baggers will figure out what you're doing. Maybe they'll ask you for a card themselves. Opportunities come in all directions. Make sure you're seen and heard as much as possible.

I was in the grocery store one day "farming" for new customers, but I wasn't having much luck. For whatever reason, it wasn't very busy. I chose my checkout line and started my way toward the cashier. Rose, the cashier, apparently had been watching me on my grocery store runs and knew what I was up to. Again, when you "farm" the grocery store, you're dressed for success with your name tag on. It's no secret that I am a real estate agent. So, Rose struck up the conversation with me regarding real estate. She told me she had been raising her grandchildren, but the youngest was about to graduate from high school and leave to attend college, and it was time for her to downsize. A 4 bedroom house was just too big for her. Guess what? Yep, I listed Rose's house for sale.

If you decide the grocery store is not your thing, there are lots of other opportunities. Consider going anywhere that people shop and might have a couple of spare minutes to chat. This could be a department store, it could be a home-improvement store, it could be a local hardware store…it could be a ton of different places.

When you've exhausted all those options, walk the local businesses in the downtown area. I'll stop in and introduce myself to small business owners and ask them if they need anything, giving them a card before I go. I also reinforce that they can contact me in the future if I can ever be of any help. All they have to do is call.

The impact of the five a day is exponential. This has not just worked for me but it has also worked for countless other agents throughout the years. People love to talk about real estate, and they love the laid-back approach.

So, go ahead. Give it a try. What's the worst they can say? No? Great! That means that you are one step closer to a yes!

Offer a Free VIP Program

Another great way to get yourself out there and network is to offer a free VIP program. Here's how this type of program works.

Create a flyer for a local business. The first time I did this was for a local home-improvement store. The flyer offered a few stellar services that I would provide free of charge for their employees as a VIP program for working with the company.

I swiped their logo from the internet and put it on the flyer, printing multiple copies with tear-off stubs at the bottom so employees could get my contact information easily. I then went into the store and asked to speak with a manager or the human resource director. I asked if they would like to hear more about this free employee benefit that they can offer, *"free"* being the keyword.

Employers are constantly searching for opportunities to offer their employees benefits for working with them. Many of these benefits cost a ton of money. So, a free employee benefit automatically grabs their attention.

I then tell them about the program, reinforcing all of the free services *and* that the company gets the credit for offering their employees this extra perk. All they need to do is hang the flyer in their employee break room. There is no other effort necessary on their part.

This program has been highly successful and can be used at a variety of different companies. You could use it with a grocery store or home-improvement store. You can use it with a box warehouse store. The options are limitless with this type of program.

What kind of benefits or services should you offer? One option is to offer discounts or help with a down-payment or closing costs.

Another is to offer simple things like going above and beyond with your customer service. Maybe you give them a bonus e-book that explains the benefits of homeownership, purchasing properties, or the process of the home purchase.

Whatever it is, your offerings need to have value in the eyes of the receiver. They don’t have to cost a lot, but they do need to hold value. That way, they’ll want it bad enough to get in contact with you.

You can also offer your VIP program exclusively to doctors, dentists, nurses, teachers, or people in or any certain profession. I have found this to be highly valuable for doctors specifically.

Doctors typically have a lot of income and need tax deductions, which real estate can help with. They may not have a ton of free time, especially if they are on call often, like surgeons and obstetricians, so the VIP program might offer time-saving benefits more than anything.

Also offer these professionals a network of vendors critical to a successful real estate deal. This includes accountants, attorneys, and other specialists who can help a buyer or seller make the best decision for them.

If you can help these individuals understand the need for real estate, they'll become your customer for life. I have doctors that I've helped purchase over 80 properties, all from printing a flyer and mailing it to them. I'd say that's a pretty good return on investment.

Who will *you* create a VIP program for? Which businesses in your area would you like to help? What professions would you enjoy working with? These are the ones you want to give a flyer first.

Identifying Influencers

After compiling a database of every single person you know, it's time to create a second database. This is what I call *the influential database.*

These are people in your community who tend to have influence over many other people. You want these people to know you as much as possible. That way, if they are ever asked if they know a real estate agent, they will refer the person to you.

Who should be placed in your influential database? People like your mayor, city council members, county council members, and any other elected officials in your local area. Individuals in these roles can have a high level of influence over numerous other people.

Also include any well-known or well-established attorneys in the area that you might be able to gain high levels of business from. Estate attorneys, divorce attorneys, and bankruptcy attorneys can all be great referral partners.

How about financial advisors and CPAs? They know a wealth of people they can send your way. Plus, real estate and increasing financial health often go hand in hand. That makes these professionals an important part of your influential database.

You may also want to include owners and managers of companies with more than 10 or 15 employees. They have influence over these employees and can definitely send you business as well.

Let's say you slowly start adding one person at a time to your database, each time you have a closing. By the end of the year, this can increase your database by 40 to 100 people.

The problem is that they *just* purchased a house from you. How long will it be before they use your services again? Remember the average starvation period? 12 years!

Trust me, if you live by this cycle, you *will* starve in the meantime. That is why your influential database is so important. It is made up of people who can continually send you business over and over and over again.

While farming in my grocery store one day, I hear someone yelling my name from far away. As I look over, it took me a moment to realize who was calling my name. He was also waving while walking toward me, trying to get my attention. With a great big smile, here comes the mayor. The mayor! He makes his way toward me and asks me how I'm doing, then asks about the real estate market. After a pleasant conversation, we said our goodbyes and he walked away. I stood there in awe. The mayor just flagged me down. *Me*...In the weeks and months to follow, not only did I get to know the mayor, I also started receiving invites from his wife to social functions and fundraisers. Some of them even in their home. That's when it really hit me how powerful my influentional database had become. I had never met the mayor before, ever!

Continuing the list, how about insurance agents? Or lenders? Even though real estate agents might refer their customers to the lender, the lender may also meet people who need representation.

The same thing goes with inspectors that you use and any other vendor throughout the process, like a roofer or anyone else. Create these relationships and set the expectation that if you send them business, you hope they send you business as well.

Once you have your influential database built, what do you send them? How do you introduce yourself? More on that in the marketing section. But first, let's talk about your closest 100.

Your Closest 100

Once you have a pretty good database put together, I always like to go back at the end of each year and identify my closest 100. This is a different category from my larger database of past customers and people that I know.

As your database reaches 5000 people or more, it becomes extremely difficult to keep in touch with all of these people regularly. It becomes overwhelming and expensive. That's why I have my closest 100 database.

Your closest 100 database is the 100 people who send you the most referrals in any given year. They send you their coworkers, family, friends, and just about anybody they can think of that needs a real estate agent.

I keep this at a tight 100 and rotate it around at the end of each year, removing people if they have not sent me business and adding people who have. My closest 100 receives regular contact. They're not only getting a quarterly email newsletter, but they're also getting a phone call from me a couple of times of the year and a CMA (comparative market analysis) to update them on the value of their property along with a handwritten note each year.

(If you want more ideas on how to keep in touch with your databases, I will teach you how to be a superstar at marketing in a future section.)

I also send out bribery gifts. I call them bribery gifts but really it's just sending them a gift of appreciation for knowing them. My most popular is my barbecue apron.

This simple white apron with one-color black printing has, by far, been the gift that has outlasted any of the others. I hear continuously that men especially love it and continue to use and wear it. Every now and then someone will send me a picture of themselves wearing the apron by the grill, even though it is now years old!

Printed on the front of the apron is my name, phone number, and slogan. That's it. Not my picture or anything else that is vain, just my information to remind them that I'm here. Every single thing I purchase and send to any customer has my name on it. Always! No exception.

By keeping this database to a manageable 100 in size, it makes it much easier and more affordable to continue to contact them. The most powerful thing I send this database is a "Just Sold!" postcard every time I have a sale.

This simple postcard has my information on it along with what I just sold and a few key details like maybe the sales price, a picture of the house if it was an all-cash sale if it sold super quickly, or any other detail that may catch their attention.

All I want to do is keep my closest 100 in touch with the market. They may receive three postcards from me in the same week and then they may go for two months without hearing from me.

I have had past customers in my closest 100 that I've run into while out and about that have stopped me and said they keep my stack of postcards. Whenever someone asks them for a real estate agent, they pass it out to them just like a business card. That is awesome!

Consider the people you would put in your top 100. Who would be on this list? Make a database for just them.

Surprise CMAs

Think about a company that you are a huge fan of. A company that keeps you coming back for more and inspires complete and total loyalty. A company that you're more than happy to tell all your friends about. What do they do that to you is a *wow* experience?

Fortunately, we can offer some of these same *wow* experiences in real estate. One of the ways I do it is by giving my customers a surprise comparative market analysis or CMA.

I do CMA's every year for my closest 100. This is another way that I can stay in touch with them on a personal level while also updating them on the value of their property. It's not as detailed as if they were putting their house on the market, but I think it still closer in value than some of the automated systems out there.

The surprise comes in when I do it for someone who did not ask for nor is expecting it. Let me give you more details.

Open houses can be a great way to find new customers. We know that most of the time, the people coming in don't buy the house that you're sitting open. Therefore, we try to convert them to a customer that might purchase another property instead.

Many times, at an open house you get a nosy neighbor or two that pop by. I don't mind the neighbors. I see them as one more opportunity to put someone in my database.

While I'm chitchatting with the nosy neighbor, I try to find out which house is theirs. Once I have their address, I can do a surprise CMA.

After the open house, I go back to the office and pull up their information through public records to get some details about their property. Then I do a full CMA.

I am not a fan of the automated system in which you click a button, and it tells you how much the house is worth. I don't think those are as accurate as a valuation prepared by a local real estate professional who knows the market. So, I do a full CMA, pulling my own comparable properties and putting them together.

I print out this beautiful CMA along with a cover letter and put it in a sealed envelope. Then I drop it off by their front door. Now when they come home from work or after being out and about, they see a package sitting on the front door. They open it and say, "Wow! That real estate agent from the open house actually took the time to tell us what our property was worth." That's the *wow* moment I am looking for.

The cover letter says something like this:

> *Thank you for coming to my open house. I thought you might be interested in knowing the estimated value of your property in today's current market. This valuation is based on data available through public records. So, if you would like a more detailed valuation of your*

property, please contact me for an appointment to come tour your house.

I believe this cover letter does a couple of things. One, it lets them know this is not an exact valuation because I have not seen their house. Two, if you're not interested in selling, they don't need to waste my time by making an appointment.

But if they *do* call and ask me to come and take a tour of their home, they're probably thinking about selling at some point. That is a hot lead.

Most of the time, they won't set up a follow-up appointment for you to tour their property. That's okay. My main goal is to hit them with a *wow* moment. This *wow* moment keeps me at the forefront of their mind.

Let's say in a few weeks they run into a friend that is thinking about selling their house. I think I have a pretty good chance of them recommending me over another agent who didn't offer a *wow* moment. I sure hope so anyway.

Every time you meet someone you could send a CMA, write it down. Next time you're in the office, do the CMA and deliver it or send it out. You'll be amazed at the results.

Creating Relationships

The point of all of these processes—building databases, reaching out to five people a day, offering a VIP program, identifying influencers, establishing your closest 100, and providing surprise CMAs—is to start creating relationships.

To be successful in real estate, or any other area of business for that matter, potential customers must begin to know, like, and trust you. These are the elements of marketing that take your business from where it is right now to where you want it to be in the future. And they all rely on your ability to create a relationship.

A real estate relationship is like most any other relationship in that you start slow. You give them the opportunity to get to know you over time versus trying to force yourself down their throat. This prevents you from overwhelming them to the point where they'd never want to use you as their service provider.

One way to begin building this type of relationship is to give without asking for anything in return. Show them that you are a real estate agent who doesn't see them as just another dollar sign. Present them with an image of you as a person who genuinely cares about their best interest.

The less they question your sincerity, and your motives, the more they will want to work with you. You become more of a trusted friend and advisor, making you someone they automatically want to come to when it comes to buying or selling property.

Even if you never earn a cent from this relationship, you can still make a great living from the people that they refer to you. Sometimes it is these secondary relationships that impact your business most.

How are you at creating relationships? Do you excel at making a connection with others or could you use a little work in this area? If you could use some work, that's okay. Sometimes simply recognizing that you're not utilizing your relationships to the best of your ability is enough to get you on the right path.

Otherwise, do what you can to start strengthening your bonds. Strive to become a true member of their team so you are the first person they think of when it comes to real estate transactions.

Strive to Connect

Another valuable thing you can do with the people you know (or will soon know) is to strive to connect them with other business professionals.

In some cases, these connections involve introducing them to people who can make the real estate transaction smoother. This could include connecting them with a local mover with a good reputation or giving the name of someone at the school where their kids will attend.

Other times, these connections may have nothing at all to do with real estate. Maybe they express concern because they don't know where to go to get their hair done so you connect them with your hairdresser or they aren't sure who to trust for child care so you give them the name of someone your friend uses.

Again, being willing to make these connections even when it doesn't benefit you helps them realize that you are genuine in your desire to help them make a smooth transition. This helps inspire loyalty because you've shown that you deserve their trust.

Taking the concept of connections even further, there may be some points in time where you connect someone with a different real estate agent.

Maybe they want to buy or sell a type of property you aren't familiar with.

It may seem foolish to refer them to someone else, but when you are willing to do this, it shows that you will put their needs before your own. Isn't this someone you want to do business with? For many, the answer is yes.

So, when they need the services you offer in the future, or if they have someone who could use them now, they are more than happy to make the referral. You become known as the consummate professional, someone who goes above and beyond to make sure people are taken care of.

Also, strive to connect professionals with each other. Let them know who you trust with *your* business, so they know that they can trust them too.

You can't win every sale, nor should you. Instead, sometimes you get further ahead by admitting when you're not the right person for the job. Being willing to point potential clients to someone who can serve them better helps your reputation more than hurts it.

In fact, taking on a deal that is outside of your area of expertise could actually land you in hot water.

So, even if you lose your commission, you've also saved yourself from a lawsuit.

Chapter Recap

- Build your database to include all the people in your area who should know you.
- Make contact with at least five new people every day, handing each one your business card.
- Offer a free VIP program for area businesses and/or individuals working in a specific profession.
- Identify influencers in your area as these are the people who can send you large quantities of work.
- List your closest 100 and make contact with them regularly.
- Provide a *wow* experience by sending surprise CMAs.
- Create relationships slowly so people learn to know, like, and trust you.
- Strive to make connections for people, even if they have nothing to do with real estate.

Chapter 5
Be a Superstar

"If your competitors start copying you, then you are doing something right!"
Jay Baer, Founder of Convince and Convert

The Power of Donuts

I have a confession. I totally stole this one. There used to be a day when it was quite common for builders and those who sat in the model center to come to our real estate offices and bribe us with donuts and cookies. It was a great excuse to get into our office and, once they were there, they could promote their products and leave flyers for us to pick up every time we grabbed a sweet treat.

One day while walking through my local grocery store, I thought, why am I not doing the same thing? I was looking for something to do to drum up more business and realized that I had several past customers (and other people that I knew) who worked for companies that had many employees. I wanted to connect with these employees and create a relationship to hopefully sell a house. Thus, the donut idea was born.

I would grab a few boxes of half-dozen donuts in the morning, then travel to two or three different companies, dropping off the donuts with my card attached to the box.

I would leave the box as a simple thank you for letting me stop by. I'd catch up with them on what was happening in their life, sharing that I hoped everyone was well. It was a wonderfully easy way for me to reconnect with people in my database.

It was also an excellent way for me to connect with future potential customers. And it all cost me less than ten dollars. Now that is some affordable marketing.

Think about the businesses you could reach out to in your area with a box of donuts every now and then. Make a list and aim to hit a couple each week. I even take them to my normal appointments I had throughout the day, places like my hair salon or doctor's office. They love it!

If you have a local business that sells specialty sweets, talk to the owner, and ask if you could get a discount by putting in a standing order every Wednesday. This allows you to support other small business owners while promoting your business, making it a win-win!

Check out bakeries, cupcake stores, chocolate stores, and any other business selling sweets locally. Larger supermarkets may also give you a discount if you order regularly. It never hurts to ask. The most they can do is say no.

Who knows? They may appreciate your business so much that they too would want to use you when they're ready to buy or sell real estate. Again, the more people you interact with, the more connections you make, the bigger your database, and the more likely you are to make a sale. All because you took the time to build a relationship.

Targeted Marketing

There are so many options these days for marketing that you could spend yourself broke in an instant.

When you are lucky enough to take a new listing, of course, you put it in the multiple listing service. It goes out to every website you could ever think of. But who is the most likely buyer?

Imagine that you take a listing for a very unique property. Let's say it's a property that also has a grass runway strip and an airport hangar attached to the house. I'm sure you can guess that your most likely buyer is someone who owns an airplane. So how do you find them? This is what we call targeted marketing and, if used correctly, it can be extremely effective in selling your property.

You can find almost any bit of information about people nowadays because we share it so freely. We share on social media and we share through our Google accounts and phones. There are all kinds of ways to get information.

Not only do *we* share it, but there are also companies that take our data and sell it. This is a big market for this because our personal data is extremely valuable.

There is a way to access this information as an individual real estate agent. You can purchase it through a company called DataAxleUSA.com, formerly known as InfoUSA.

I have personally used this company for over 30 years and have found it to be extremely effective and accurate. Just go to their website, input the criteria that you're looking for, and they will tell you how many leads you can get and the cost.

If you purchase the mailing list, you can instantly download it to your computer and convert the addresses into labels or upload them to the marketing company that you've hired to send information about the property. Bingo! That's how you find people who own airplanes.

That's also how you find people who own horses or enjoy camping and many other hobbies and interest that each of us has. This is where you can purchase lists of divorce attorneys, doctors, financial advisors, and so on. Once you master targeted marketing, you can sell anything because you will know exactly where to find the perfect buyer.

Sometimes it isn't as easy to identify your target market. The property isn't as unique, so there isn't a stand-out demographic for your ideal buyer. What do you do then?

Try to visualize what type of person would get the most enjoyment out of the property. Would a younger couple be happier there or an older couple who is ready to retire? Is it a good home for kids? Pets? Based on the amenities it provides, who would find it most appealing.

Think also about the location of the property. Is it near a business that hires thousands of workers for a specific type of role? This might be a good demographic to reach out to.

Which school district is it in? If the home is suitable for children, market people with kids in that age range. Or maybe it's near a ball field. That would be a good target market as well.

Put yourself in the mind of the ideal buyer and seek to identify who that person is. The more you understand their likes and dislikes, the easier it becomes to tailor your marketing campaign directly to them.

Social Media

Have you ever tracked how much time you spend on social media each week? Social media platforms like Facebook, Instagram, LinkedIn, Snapchat, and YouTube have a lot of impact and most of us use them daily. How does that affect your business? Think about what kind of a return you could get from these options. Yes, I do believe that it helps keep us in front of our customers. And we can connect with people that we might not have otherwise been able to connect with if we were not on social media.

It's like going to a networking event and running into someone who knows someone else that you want to meet. They can be the connector to introduce you. Social media serves the same purpose.

I love how social media keeps us in touch with each other. I love how we can follow what's going on in everyone's lives and see the changes and new exciting things so on by simply scrolling through our news feed.

That said, these platforms can also breed negativity. These days, it seems that if you don't agree with someone else's idea, they will berate you and your posts.

When the negativity gets too much, I take a *social media fast*. I take a break. It could be for a week, it could be for a month, it could be for a day. Sometimes you just have to go offline and do other things.

Even with all the negativity, social media still has enough pros to outweigh the cons. One, it would be virtually impossible to go see all the people you connect with in person. Social media allows you to stay in touch virtually, from the comfort of your office or home.

Two, being front and center in your customers' minds is where you always want to be and social media plays a big part in that. Your posts appear in their feeds, reminding them that you're there when they're ready to buy or sell. But, as with all things, there comes a catch.

If you spend a lot of time on social media, you must wonder about your return on investment. Ask around and find out how many real estate professionals have sold a house just through social media.

This also involves keeping in check how much time it's taking from us versus how much we're getting in return. If you're worth an hourly rate of $35 an hour, will you see a return on investment of $35 for that hour you just spent online?

If not, maybe it's time to outsource this particular marketing effort. Maybe it's time to have a definite plan in place when going online. Let me give you some tips.

In my opinion, using social media to promote our real estate business is no different than any other drip campaign we can launch to keep in touch with our customer base. It is just one more tool in the toolbox to assist us. We also need to ensure that it is not the *only* tool in the toolbox.

What do you think could have more of an impact on your customers or be more memorable: receiving a handwritten notecard in their mailbox or you commenting on one of their posts?

It's common to get caught up in the social media frenzy and I do believe that when you own a business and you are in customer service, you want to meet as many people as possible. Social media is a vital part of that plan. But it's only *one* piece of the plan.

So, make sure you track how much time you spend on social media. Give yourself a time-based budget. In other words, limit your time spent daily on social media sites. Decide upfront whether that time is per platform or for all platforms combined.

Make a plan and stick to it. Set a timer when you go online so you don't get distracted. This helps you not lose track of your time to the point where it gets away from you.

The next issue is deciding which sites to be on. Where you choose to spend your time should coincide with where your customer base spends the majority of *their* time.

Are most of your customers on Instagram or do they tend to hang out on Facebook? It's not going to do you any good to be on a social media platform that is different than your target audience.

Let's say your customer base is on Facebook. Facebook can email you daily and tell you who's birthday it is. So, you go online to wish these people a happy birthday.

If there are many people with the same birthdate, craft one message and post it on each one. This can save you a lot of time versus thinking about how to make each greeting unique.

It also keeps you from getting distracted and going elsewhere on the site, spending even more time.

Otherwise, you may end up searching through your timeline to see who else you need to wish a happy birthday or get caught up looking at your alerts or seeing who commented on your posts. Before you know it, hours have passed by and you have not completed your other work.

Another great option is to use a social media management platform so you can see all your social media in one place. These platforms also give you an all-encompassing view of what's going on with your posts and responses.

I use Hootsuite, although there are lots of options available. With a service like this, you can schedule posts for the future. This is helpful if you want to create your weekly or monthly posts all in one sitting. It's also good if you are going to be off work for a vacation or surgery, enabling you to continue to post during that time.

Social media management services also allow you to see past results of your posts and comments, just like you would if you were in each individual social media account. I love the analytical data it provides and saves you tons of time from being distracted from other people's posts.

It also keeps you from a lot of the negativity that exists online. For this factor alone, it may be worth it. Check out Hootsuite.com.

Your Online Reputation

Do you know what people are saying about you online? Have you checked lately? Along the same lines, have you ever thought about how often you should be reviewing your online reputation to ensure that it matches the same reputation that you're working hard to create in person?

In today's world of Yelp, Google, and all the other internet-based review sites, it's clear that a lot of people turn to the online world when they are unhappy. Most of the time, I think they just want to be heard and know the internet will deliver.

But what happens if someone recommends you to their neighbor and that neighbor goes online and finds that someone had a not so happy experience with you previously? It may not even be a true rendition of what happened. Regardless, they're not going to be excited to work with you if they believe what they've read online.

In most cases, these potential sellers will decide to take a different route and call a competitor. You've lost their business. The crazy thing is that you didn't even realize you had a chance to gain their business, to begin with. You lost it before you knew it existed, all because of the online reputation.

Automation has dramatically changed the way we do things. One way you can put automation to work for you when it comes to your online reputation is to ask the internet to notify you every time someone posts about you and your business. You can do this with Google Alerts.

This service sends you an email when your name or your business's name is being discussed online. You get to decide whether this email is sent the moment new content about you is posted, or you can set it up to notify you once a day or once a week at most. There are so many ways that you can use Google Alerts when it comes to managing your online reputation, but first, let me explain how to set it up.

Visit Google.com/alerts and, in the search bar, type the words you want to create an alert for. It might be something like your name and the location that you serve as a real estate agent.

For example, my alert would be for "Cynthia DeLuca real estate central Florida." I don't just use my name because I don't want to be notified when something is posted online for every Cynthia

DeLuca that exists today. I only want the posts that are related to me, the real estate agent in my geographical area.

Next, click on "Show Options" and you get to decide how often you want to search to be emailed to you. I chose once a week, but it's up to you how often you want to be notified. Your other options are instantly and daily.

You also get to choose what language and region you want alerts for, as well as whether you want to be emailed all results or only the best results. Once you've populated these fields, click on "Create Alert" and you're done. You will now receive an email with your desired keywords in the time interval you've selected.

Now, let's say that, sometime down the road, you receive an email that shows a new review has been posted. You click on that link and it takes you to a website where someone posted a negative review. What do you do from here? To preserve your reputation, I have found the following is the best way to handle online reviews.

First, I try to reach out to the customer offline, meaning that I'm going to pick up the phone and give them a call or try to contact them in whatever way I know. Once I get a hold of them, I let them know that I saw their review and I'm sorry that they feel that way. I work through their feelings with them and strive to help resolve their issues.

If we can resolve the problem, I ask them if they will kindly remove their review within 24 hours. Some will say yes and agree to remove it. Others might say yes and never remove it. Either way, it doesn't hurt to ask.

After 24 hours, I go back online to review their post. If they did not alter it, change it, or remove it, I respond to their negative review in a professional and courteous way. My response generally looks something like this:

> *I am sorry that you feel this way. After reaching out to you to discuss this issue, I'm glad that we were able to come up with a resolution to resolve the situation for you. If there's anything else I can be of assistance with, please feel free to reach out and contact me. I look forward to working with you in the future.*

The reason for this response is not for the person who posted the review. It's really for the thousands of people that will potentially see that post over the next few years.

Issuing a response shows others that you stayed professional. That you took care of whatever you could, and that you responded instead of ignoring the upset customer. Sometimes, this can get you further than a five-star review.

Google Alerts can be your eyes around the internet, notifying you of any post that could affect your reputation. What other searches could you set up? What about one for your brokerage company or broker? Are there any others you can think of?

The nice thing about Google Alerts is that you can set up as many as you like. You can also go in at any time and change, add, or delete your alerts.

There are *so* many ways you can use Google Alerts and I'd love to hear about how you use yours! Go to my website at www.CynthiaDeLuca.com and send me a message. Tell me how you use yours in a way that helps you better manage your online reputation.

How Much Are You Investing?

If you have ever opened a business, you know that it comes with quite an expense. One of those expenses is related to marketing, or the advertising of your business. So, how much have you committed to investing in your marketing efforts?

The general rule of thumb is to commit between 20 and 25% of your gross revenue into your marketing budget. What does this mean? For every dollar in commission income that you receive, you should be putting $0.25 to the side for your marketing, to generate more dollars down the road.

There are many ways to market yourself and your business. Here are a few to consider:

- Newspaper ads
- Neighborhood newsletters
- Chamber of Commerce website
- Church newsletters
- TV ads
- Radio ads
- Billboards
- Bus benches
- Social media promotional ads
- Market updates mailed to a geographic neighborhood
- Google Ads
- Local sponsorships of kids' sports teams, school events, etc.
- Sponsoring local events such as festivals and 5ks
- Host free seminars for buyers, investors, etc.

- Purchase leave-behinds (pens, keychains, and other freebies containing your name and contact info)
- Offer free home valuations
- Create a YouTube channel where you post videos highlighting your local area, with you as the expert and host
- Write real estate articles for local magazines or newspapers
- Write guest posts for other people's blogs
- Join local organizations to meet new people
- Guest star on a podcast (check out CrowdQuestion.com to find podcasters looking for guests)
- Wrap your car or use car magnets
- Every Door Direct Mail marketing (see USPS.com for more details)
- Join Facebook groups with your interest and comment regularly
- Door knocking
- And the list goes on and on…

What about ways to keep in touch with your existing database? We need to do that as well.

Some professionals are tempted to only market when business is down. However, you should constantly be advertising yourself as a real estate agent. This keeps your sales funnel full of leads, increasing the number who make it to the bottom, resulting in a closing.

Want a detailed plan of ways to keep in touch with the people in your database? Just go to my website, www.CynthiaDeLuca.com, and you can download a free follow up plan. For this item, make sure you use the coupon code "Standout". That way you can download the item for free, just for you reading this book, my standout crowd.

Your Resume

You can always tell when a co-worker is headed to a closing. They are dressed fancy, in a good mood, and maybe even bought a box of donuts for the office. I've never really understood why a real estate professional puts so much effort into the end of the transaction.

The closing is the day you become unemployed, isn't it? You've done your job and now you're closing. Hooray! Yes, you're getting paid and that's a wonderful feeling. But now you are also out of work and must go seek new employment. Let that sink in for a moment.

If we're seeking employment, and we constantly are, we have to think like a job seeker. Typically, someone who is looking for a job has a resume. Do *you* have a resume?

You need to have a resume available for buyers, sellers, people stopping at your open houses, and just about anywhere else that you're promoting yourself and telling people you want to be hired. What goes on your resume?

Your past experience is a good thing to include on your resume, as long as you don't overdo it. You want to show a proven track record without being self-centered.

If you are brand new to the industry and, therefore, haven't been involved in many transactions, rely on the experience of your brokerage company. You picked them, so hopefully, they come with good experience and a good reputation that will make you proud to put them on your resume.

Don't be afraid to also include past experiences, not in the real estate field. There is always something you learned in a previous experience that makes you a better agent. Draw on that and consider how it benefits them, both through the transaction and through working with you.

Be sure to connect the dots for them. If you are too vague, people will wonder what your non-real estate experience matters. Yet, if you explain the skills you learned in that role *and* how they better equip you to buy and sell property, it will all make perfect sense.

For example, if you used to work in construction, this says that you know more than the average person when it comes to a property's foundation or structure. If you worked in customer service, it says that you understand the importance of delivering a good product or service.

Any education that you have that's above the standard requirements of your state licensing should also be listed on your resume. Hold any designations or certifications? Make sure you note those.

Also, take a moment to explain what each designation is and how it helps the customer versus just putting a jumbled mess of letters that they don't understand.

If someone isn't familiar with the field, seeing a designation like CIPS doesn't mean a thing. Conversely, if you share that this stands for Certified International Property Specialist and means that you have additional training in international real estate transactions, it becomes plain as day. It also clearly differentiates your areas of expertise (your niche).

On a typical resume, there is usually a spot for references. I translate this into not just offering a reference, but more of a testimonial. Gather a few good testimonials from past customers or other people that know you and will give you a character testimonial. Include these on your resume and share their references with potential customers.

Remember that we are *always* seeking employment. And if we're seeking employment, we need to be hirable. This means always being ready and willing to offer a resume to anyone who could potentially want to work with us when buying or selling a property.

Put yours together so you can grab it at a moment's notice. This shows that you're prepared, organized, and ready to take on the job.

Want to see a sample resume? Download one from my website at www.CynthiaDeLuca.com, in the shop.

Throw Away the Recipe Cards

Recipes are great. If you follow them correctly, you will end up with the same dish each and every time.

While this is good in the kitchen, it's not necessarily going to help you stand out in the real estate market.

If you want to set yourself apart from your competitors, you must be unique. You must be true to yourself, your personality, and your style. Trying to be like everyone else will make you, well, like everyone else.

Look at it this way. If 10 candy bars were lying in front of you and they all looked the same, which one would you pick? It wouldn't matter. Because each one is the same as the next, there is no compelling reason to choose one over the other.

This can be the death of you in the real estate world. If potential customers can't differentiate you from every other agent in the field, it becomes a random draw. You'll only get buyers and sellers to do business with you out of luck. How long do you think you'll stay in business with this approach?

Figure out what makes you different. Specifically, find out what makes you better than your competition. These are the factors you want to highlight in your marketing efforts.

Maybe you provide better customer service than any other agent in your area. In that case, talk about how you go above and beyond for your customers.

Help them visualize how wonderful their life will be if they choose you as their real estate professional.

This is also a good time to talk about your niche. If you have more experience or education in a specific sector of real estate, share this information. Let potential buyers know where you excel. Make it easy for them to contact you if they need assistance in the same area.

Your primary goal should be the filet mignon when everyone else is serving burgers. Or the swordfish when everyone else is offering tilapia. Show the people in your database that you follow your own recipes. Recipes that can't be found elsewhere because they are unique to you.

Pay Attention to Trends

If you want to succeed in real estate, you must be relevant. Put another way, people must want what you have to sell.

One of the easiest ways to figure out what people want is to pay attention to trends. Get curious and seek to learn what people want most *right now* when it comes to real estate.

A good tool for this purpose is Google Trends (https://trends.google.com/). On this site, you can tailor your search to a specific region, timeframe, and category. This enables you to be as broad or specific as you like.

To use Google Trends, enter your desired keywords into the search bar and it will provide related topics and queries. For example, if you search "real estate," you may see related topics such as real estate brokers or commercial property. Related queries might include the real estate market for that year or what specific terms mean in real estate.

This is important because it tells you not only what topics are being talked about most—giving you the opportunity to chime in as well—but it also tells you what type of information people are searching for as well. Provide the answers in your online materials and you can quickly begin to increase your search result rank.

Including a blog on your website gives you a place to post articles that includes the most recently trending keywords. Google likes blogs too. The more you post, the higher you'll show in the search results when someone is actively looking for your services.

You can also use trending keywords on your web pages. However, if you take this approach, you will need to update your site regularly so that it continues to stay current. This is why a blog is often a better option. It allows you to include the keywords in your content without continuously having to redo your website.

Once you know what people are searching for most, you can also use it as an opportunity to write a guest post on that topic. Ask a high-traffic blog or online publication to post your article. Include a bio at the bottom with a link back to your real estate website.

Google likes backlinks as much as it likes keywords. These are the links on other pages that link back to your site. The more of these you have on reputable online sites, the more credible you are in Google's eyes. The more credible you are to Google, the higher your rank.

If you do want to post on a site that is not your own, it is always recommended to reach out to that site first. Let them know what you want to write about and get their approval. If you don't take this step, you risk spending hours to craft the perfect piece only to have no one who is willing to publish it.

Reaching out beforehand also gives that site the opportunity to tell you if they want you to approach the topic from a specific angle. For example, if you want *Parents Magazine* to publish your piece, they may want you to write specifically to single parents or parents with small children at home. Knowing this from the very beginning prevents you from having to back in and majorly edit your article because it is not quite what they want.

Site publishers also typically have a good handle on the topics that are trending most with their readers. Let them tell you what those topics are so you don't have to do as much research or, worse yet, guess.

Multiply Your Exposure

Do you know what makes a multipurpose tool so great? For one price, you get a screwdriver (both Phillips and flathead), pliers, a knife, a saw, wire cutters, and a bottle opener. This one tool provides the ability to tackle a variety of projects. This is also what you should strive for with your marketing.

Ideally, you want to choose marketing options that serve multiple purposes. This increases your exposure exponentially without having to put in a ton of additional work.

For example, if you do have a blog on your real estate website, constantly coming up with new topics to write about isn't always easy. If you struggle with this too much, you might decide to not write at all, leaving this portion of your website to go stale.

What many don't realize is that you can always take an old blog and refresh it so it looks shiny and new. You don't want to simply republish it because this could hurt your ranking with Google. But if you just change around a few words and add a new section or two, you've got an entirely new article. This improves your rank, giving you more exposure while requiring minimal effort.

Another option is to post a blog on your website, then send an email to your database letting them know it's there. Encourage them to share it if they know someone who could benefit from the information you provide. In this case, they multiply your exposure for you. And they do so in a way that helps you reach people you wouldn't normally reach.

Influencers have the same ability. Find someone who is already killing it with your target market and see if they would be willing to endorse your real estate business. Some may do it if you endorse them in return. Others charge a fee for this service.

The one thing to be careful of if you take this approach is that the influencer has a brand or reputation that you are okay being connected with. If they endorse you, their name and yours are now intertwined. This also means that if they fall from grace, you will likely fall with them.

So, don't just use someone who has a lot of followers or connections without doing your research. Read the things they post online to see if you're okay with their message and the way they speak.

For example, some influencers use a lot of cuss words. Even if their followers are okay with this, it may not be the image you want to present. Reaching out to an influencer with cleaner language might be more in line with your brand.

Essentially, you want to try to look for the marketing efforts that go after the big fish who will bring the little fish with them. This enables you to fill your net with one swoop versus having to dip it into the water again and again and again.

Chapter Recap

- Providing sweet treats is a great way to market yourself in a way that most people don't mind.

Continued….

- Use targeted marketing so you get yourself and your properties in front of the most likely buyer.
- Social media is a great marketing tool, just limit your time on them, and be sure to select the platforms used most by your customers.
- Keep your finger on your online reputation by setting up Google Alerts to notify you whenever someone reviews you and your services.
- Always have a resume handy for the times when you run into someone who is looking to hire a real estate agent.
- Remember that while recipes are good in the kitchen, you'll get much further ahead as an agent if you focus on what makes you individual and unique.
- Pay attention to the latest trends so you know how to be more relevant to your customers.
- Find ways to multiply your exposure with your marketing efforts, giving you more bang for your buck.

Section 3

The Nitty-Gritty

Chapter 6
All Systems Go!

"Alone we can do so little; together we can do so much."
Helen Keller

Systems are an important part of any business, especially in real estate. We are constantly pulled in every direction. Without consistent systems, something might get missed, left behind, or just forgotten altogether.

You Can't Do It All

Do you have a pile sitting on your desk that, no matter how much extra time you seem to find in a day, it continues to just sit there? There are probably things in it that are important and need to get done, but you just keep staring at them thinking you will get to it eventually.

Or maybe you feel overwhelmed lately. There's just so much to do and not enough time to do it. Have you taken a vacation in the past six months? A real vacation with no email and no phone?

If you feel like there's never enough time in the day to get everything done, it might be time to delegate.

The independent contractor's brain typically has a difficult time letting go of stuff and giving it to someone else. But delegating office tasks—especially the ones you do not enjoy or the ones that you're not really making much money doing—can be very freeing. That is truly how you can build the life that you want, one with this work-life balance that so many people talk about.

How do you delegate, who do you delegate to, and how do you know that the tasks you delegate are going to be completed correctly?

We all know that our time is worth something right? But do we know *what* it's worth? Not always. And if we don't know what our time is worth, how can we ever decide if something is worth doing ourselves?

In *The 4-Hour Workweek*, the popular author Timothy Ferriss says, "Never automate something that can be eliminated, and never delegate something that can be automated or streamlined. Otherwise, you waste someone else's time instead of your own, which now wastes your hard-earned cash."

So, the first task at hand is to make a decision. This involves asking a few critical questions:

- Does this task have value?
- What would happen if it never were accomplished?
- Would it adversely affect my career or income?

If you answer that it would NOT affect you in a negative way, maybe elimination is the answer. Don't do it.

The next question you would ask yourself is: if I *can't* eliminate this task because it will help me accomplish my goals and lead me to a career of my dreams, can it be automated? Can I put it on auto-pilot and accomplish it automatically over time?

For instance, if you send postcards to your database six holidays a year, can you schedule this to happen automatically? Of course, you can. There are plenty of companies that will do that for you. I use ExpressCopy.com, but there are plenty of options to consider.

There are so many ways we can automate stuff. From paying bills to scheduling our robot vacuum, just look around you. There are lots of things that can be automated.

If the task can't be eliminated or automated, then ask yourself whether it can be delegated. Can someone else besides you do that task?

Believe it or not, there are lots of smart people in this world. Even if you are really good at something, it may not be the best use of your time. This is especially true if your hourly net worth is higher than what you can pay someone else to take care of that task for you.

As an example, I am very tech-savvy and have a degree in graphic design. I could absolutely build a website, design a logo, even design my book covers. Easy peasy. But I don't do any of these things. I hire freelancers on Fiverr.com and UpWork.com instead. Why?

Because I paid $30 to have my entire website designed in WordPress. Thirty dollars! I would have spent hours creating that site and overthinking the process. If your time is worth $50 an hour, you better be able to design your entire website in half an hour, otherwise, you've just lost money. Now, do you see why it's so important to know what your time is worth?

When I hired my first assistant, I'd been in real estate for about three years. I decided it was time because, well, quite frankly, that's when I realized I fell asleep in my office. I was working so many hours and was exhausted. I woke up about 4 a.m., realized I had dozed off, and made a commitment at that moment to hire help!

Time to hire an assistant. But at that point in time, we didn't have virtual assistants. We didn't have options like Upwork and Fiverr and whatnot. So, the problem was that I had to hire a "real person" and they had to come and sit in my office every day. I had to be responsible for providing them a steady income, even when my income was not steady.

As you know, there are a lot of ups and downs in our flow of income. I always say, one day we're eating peanut butter and jelly, the next week we're eating steak, and the week after that we're back to peanut butter and jelly. We just have no consistency.

So, the challenge was that I was taking on a lot of responsibility. It was a very difficult decision, but I hired an assistant. She worked 20 hours a week for me in the beginning and it was the best thing I ever did.

The National Association of REALTORS® offers a lot of statistics. One shows that when you hire someone and allow them to take stuff off your plate, your income increases. Did you hear me? Your income actually increases!

I believe in the philosophy of eyeball to eyeball. (Some people call it belly to belly, which is basically the same thing.) This means that if you're not in front of your customer at a listing appointment, showing property, networking, or doing things like that—if you're not eyeball to eyeball with people—which could be online as well, you're not making money.

We do a lot of paperwork. Do we make any more money by doing this paperwork? No. It's a necessary part of the process, but it's not something that makes us more money. So, the question is, could we pay somebody else to do those things? Of course! By knowing what your time is worth, you will then know if it makes sense to delegate that task.

We should be working around 2,000 hours per year, assuming that we're all working 40-hour workweeks 50 weeks per year, with a two-week vacation. Let's say that your goal is $50,000 in income for the year. This does not take into account IRS taxes, expenses, etc. This is just looking at raw numbers of what you want to earn annually.

At $50,000 a year, and we know we only have 2,000 hours to work because we can't create more time, your hourly rate is $25 an hour ($50,000 ÷ 2,000 = $25). Knowing this, are there certain tasks that you could have completed for you that will cost less than $25 an hour to pay somebody else to do? Probably. Let me tell you how I identify these tasks with my delegation worksheet.

On a pad of paper, draw a line straight down the middle. On the left-hand side, write down everything you do on a regular basis. We check emails, we search new listings, we send postcards, we lead generate, we go on listing appointments, we research properties, and do a CMA. The list goes on and on. (Some people include the amount of time they spend on each item when creating this list. That's up to you. I don't, but you can.)

The very first time you do this, it takes about two weeks to make sure you've included everything you do on the list, and you should redo it every six months or so. After you've spent a couple of weeks and developed a good solid list, go back and ask who else could be doing each job. I always do this by position versus by person.

For instance, there are assistants. There are virtual assistants, freelancers, marketing assistants, and transaction coordinators. There are also buyer's agents and listing agents. There are quite a few options when it comes to assistant-type roles.

You want to try to figure out who else could be taking care of these items for you, eliminating as much as you can from your own plate.

Maybe one of the items on your list is to check emails. Who could do that for you? An assistant?

Are you comfortable letting someone else check your emails? Personally, I am not, so I take care of this task myself. But if you're okay with this, that's great. It could be an item that you assign out.

What about hiring an assistant to check the hot sheet of new listings daily? Right now, it's probably you or a buyer's agent performing this task. But it doesn't have to be. Eliminate yourself from the process, automate it, then delegate it to someone else.

When it comes to postcards, I've automated this process in addition to hiring a virtual assistant. I've used a company called Express Copy for probably at least 18 years. They have a calendar, and you can go on and upload your own design, or you can pick from one of their roughly 250 templates and send out big or small postcards. They have a bunch of different options to choose from.

What I love about it is, before the year even begins in January, I've already uploaded all of my marketing materials for the entire year. I don't have to wait until an event occurs to go in and create my order. It is already done for me.

All you have to do is upload your database, put in your credit card number, pick the date on the calendar that you want them to mail the postcards, and you don't have to think about it again. They just send you an email that says your postcards went out and life is good, right?

That's the automation process. And you can even pay a virtual assistant to upload your postcards and schedule them for you. Life is good!

What if you need to research properties? Let's say that you're going on a listing appointment, so you need to research the property, pull up public records, etc. An assistant can do that.

I have a virtual assistant who does this for me. To make the process easier, I use a free Chrome browser plugin called Screencastify. Screencastify records your screen in video form. This is helpful if you plan to have a virtual assistant research property for you because you can go in and show them the steps they need to take with a short 5 or 10-minute video. If you don’t like Screencastify, don’t worry, there are plenty of options out there. I also use free Logitech software as well. You could even use a free Zoom account.

The beauty of this is that a lot of virtual assistants arc not living near you. Maybe they're not even living in the U.S. Because of this, they may not understand the process. If you record a quick video and send it to them, they can watch that video 100 times if they need to, but they know step by step exactly what you want them to do.

And if they don't do it the way you want, you need to fire them. Unfortunately, firing a virtual assistant has to happen sometimes. But anyway, Screencastify is a lifesaver because you can just give them a quick tutorial, like, "Hey, create this quick spreadsheet for me" or "Please do this" and it gives them a solid idea of what you want.

Plus, if you don't actually show them, they won't always understand what it is you want. And they won't always tell you that they don't understand, making for a frustrating process for both of you.

Also understand that virtual assistants are typically paid by the job, not the hour. So, they're watching YouTube, but they're also creating my spreadsheet. I don't care as long as the work gets done and it's done right, within the price and time agreed.

Let's talk about a CMA for a minute. Who could prepare a CMA for us? An assistant could do that too. Absolutely. Once it's done, review it and make sure it's accurate. If you're not comfortable delegating the CMA, there's still plenty of other stuff the V.A. can do. These include preparing the docs, filling in the listing, and more.

Okay, back to our task list. When going through the items on your list, pay attention to the title or job description that shows up the most. This is your next hire.

Then take each of the line items that you've attributed to this position and that becomes your job description. In the case of a virtual assistant, this may include sending postcards, researching properties, preparing a CMA, filling in the listing agreement, etc.

It might look something like this:

Research property info	Assistant
Fill in Listing Agreement	Assistant
Check Emails	Me
Network at Chamber Events	Me
Get extension signed on listing	Assistant
Follow up with buyers	Me
Solicit feedback froim showings	Assistant
Fill in Contract offer	Assistant
Sign offer with buyers	Me
Social Media posts	Assistant
Send postcards out	Assistant
Marketing flyer for open house	Assistant

With your bulleted list in hand, you can start the hiring process. Begin looking for a virtual assistant who offers the services you want. Interview potential candidates and pick one. Then let go and allow them to do these tasks.

Here's what generally happens. We delegate all of these duties, it's a month down the road and we're super successful. The virtual assistants we've hired are on their way, they're working right and doing what we ask, and we think, "Gosh, why didn't I do this sooner?"

I also pay a virtual assistant to manage my CRM system, which I hate to do. How much does it cost me? Around $3.30 an hour. And he supports his entire family in Bangladesh on that. This virtual assistant doesn't just work for me; he works for other people too. And we've gotten to know each other over time.

One other thing I'll comment on is that this assistant has different holidays and different religious holidays than I do in the U.S. So if you hire someone living far away, be very respectful of this. If you need something done within a week or a day, make sure it's not a holy day or some other day that they are not working.

You can take the same approach with some of your personal obligations. Maybe you don't have the time or desire to clean your house after your long days at work. Could you pay somebody less than $25 an hour to do that for you? Probably. (If you have kids, you can likely get them to do it for much less than that!)

What about meal prep? That's a big thing right now. My sister-in-law, she doesn't cook at all anymore. She gets meals delivered for her and her husband. And she eliminated grocery shopping at the same time by hiring a meal service.

We are all wired for certain things. So, you have that pile on your desk. Yeah, that's what you're not wired to do. In other words, those things that you don't want to do, that you don't find enjoyment in doing, they just kind of sit there and pile up. Those are the things that you want to hire help with.

I know speakers who hire people to do all of their schedules and arrangements and hotels and all that stuff. I've considered doing the same because I don't enjoy sitting down and researching hotels or trying to figure that stuff out. So, it just depends on what you're looking for them to do.

Even if you are using specific programs, you can get a virtual assistant to use these programs for you.

If you hire a bookkeeper, for example, they can work within your QuickBooks software.

If you have the money, you can hire anyone to do anything for you. Currently, almost every restaurant and fast-food chain delivers. You've got Uber Eats and GrubHub that deliver. No more driving to pick up dinner. And it doesn't stop there. There's a ton of stuff you can hire out. You've got grocery delivery. You've got Amazon, who delivers just about everything, maybe even groceries!

Amazon started delivering fresh items in the Orlando area, which they've been doing for years in Seattle, where my brother lives. My brother showed me how amazing it is. In less than an hour, they're at your door with milk and eggs and whatever else you ordered. Wow!

You get the idea. You can delegate whatever it is you don't enjoy, including any items sitting in that pile on your desk.

How many virtual assistants have I gone through, that I've had to fire, let go, release, or whatever you want to call it? Let's answer that question by saying that, when this occurs, I blame it on me. In other words, I did not hire the right person or give the right instructions, which is why I'm a big fan of Screencastify.

I mentioned that I hired a virtual assistant to do my whole website design for $30. All of my book covers were done on Fiverr. My audiobook cover was on Fiverr. I don't have to think about any of that stuff. I just tell them what I want.

You can literally pay somebody to write a book for you. Ghostwriters are everywhere on Fiverr. I have to be honest, I wrote all my books, so I don't understand that process. My first book, I dictated years ago. I always start my books with voice text. Then I go from there to the written word and do all the editing after that, though I do pay a professional editor (again, delegating). So, when I'm done with a book, I send it to my editor, and she kind of cuts it all up and fixes it for me.

You don't even have to write your own video scripts, blogs, or any other content. People can write all that stuff for you. Politicians don't write their own speeches. You should have this benefit too.

I know people who pay virtual assistants or freelancers to copywrite. A professional copywriter writes material that invokes a response. A friend of mine owns a brokerage that pays a copywriter on Fiverr to write the descriptions for all their listings. They go in and create the emotion to encourage the sale.

This person looks at the pictures, looks at the description of the property, and then writes an article that fits in the public remarks. All of this can be done through a shared folder, such as DropBox.

That's one thing that sets my friend apart, having a professional copywriter write every one of their MLS descriptions. I think it's brilliant.

Sometimes it's not necessarily that you don't want to do it, but more so that somebody else could do it better. That's another way you could look at it. The internet really has opened up opportunities up for us, and the sky is the limit with finding talented people.

Now that we've delegated, we don't just take those newly open spots in our time and go sit on the beach, right? We end up filling them with other things. That's why it's necessary to repeat this process every 6 months or so. So what will you delegate first?

Who Are You?

Have you ever taken a personality test to discover your unique characteristics or to get a better idea of what you're wired to do? The results can be truly enlightening. They help you understand why you do the things you do and why you think the way that you think.

There is a multitude of different personality styles. Some people are strategic, whereas others are more of a free thinker. Some rely more on logic or data to make decisions and others tend to act based on emotion.

A personality test can help you identify what makes you act and react. It also tells you the ways in which you tend to solve problems or deal with difficult situations. Just having an understanding of your thought and behavior patterns makes it easier to realize why you think and act as you do.

Having access to this information also shines a light on how you tend to interact with others. Do you tend to be a team player or are you more of an authoritarian? Knowing this about yourself helps you realize how you may come across to your colleagues and clients.

Another reason why you'd want to take a personality test is to identify your strengths *and* your weaknesses. It tells you what you are naturally good at, as well as the areas you are likely to struggle.

When you do hire help, like an assistant or virtual assistant, you always want to hire for your weaknesses. You don't want to hire someone exactly like you or that knows how to do what you do, you want to hire someone that's excited to tackle that pile on your desk.

I would encourage you to take a Myers-Briggs (or whatever you have available) if you've never done one before. This test operates under the assumption that there are 16 different personality types. Your answers to the questions will determine which types are most applicable to you.

For example, some people are naturally outgoing (extroverts) and others like to stick to themselves (Introverts). Some people are more focused on reality (Sensing) and others are more imaginative or abstract (Intuitive). The other personality types assess whether you're more of a Thinker or a Feeler and if you Judge or if you Perceive.

Once your answers are compiled, you are given a four-letter code that signifies your individual personality type. For example, if you are an INFJ, it means that you are introverted, intuitive, feeling, and judging. In simple terms, this means that you rely strongly on your intuition, that you need time alone to recharge, and that emotion is often more important to you than facts.

By default, this means that your strengths include being sensitive to the thoughts and feelings of others, you have a lot of creativity, and that you strive for idealistic things in life.

Identifying that you are an INFJ also gives you a few clues about your most likely weaknesses. One is that you may find yourself too sensitive in certain situations. Another is having expectations so high, they simply can't be met, or disliking confrontation to the point where you're always afraid to disagree.

The more you realize these things about yourself, the more you know where you could use a little help. It also gives you an idea of what you can do to begin on your weaknesses, making you a better person and real estate agent as a result. There are a few different online sites that offer the Myers-Briggs for free.

Tony Robbins also offers a free personality test on his website. This is slightly different than the Myers-Briggs in that it separates personality types into four general quadrants:

- **D**ominance
- **I**nfluence

- Steadiness
- Conscientious

Thus, it is called a DISC personality test.

Under each quadrant is a series of personality traits matching that style. If you rank high in dominance, for example, this means that you are direct, results-oriented, decisive, competitive, and a problem solver. If you are conscientious, you are analytical, diplomatic, precise, compliant, and objective.

This test will also help you identify the way you think, behave, and interact with others. Check it out at https://www.tonyrobbins.com/disc/ if you want to see where you fall within these styles.

Setting Up Vendor Teams

When you expand your team, it does not have to be just people that you hire around you to work for you. Also consider your vendor team, or everyone who assists you in your transaction. This includes your inspectors, title company, lenders, and so on.

These people can make or break your transactions. They can also make or break your reputation. You want to make sure you use (and work) with good, reputable vendors that don't require a lot of oversight or headache.

It's not always the cheapest vendor that's the best for your client. In fact, most of the time it is the exact opposite.

Make sure you interview your vendors once a year. Seek to gain a thorough understanding of their beliefs and how they treat customers. Are they willing to call your customer directly or go through the hoops necessary to make your deals work?

You definitely want to work with vendors who appreciate and understand you. It’s also important to choose vendors that you trust with your clients.

Take some time to set up a solid vendor team. A team that helps you continue to increase your success because they provide the level of service you want and need.

A list of vendors that you might want to consider having on your team includes:

- Lenders
- Mortgage brokers and bankers
- Inspectors (home, roof, gas, septic, and well)
- Electrician
- Plumber
- HVAC company
- Title company

- Real estate attorney
- Property manager
- Homeowners insurance and dwelling policy coverage for your investors

When assembling this team, pay attention to the superstars. Identify the people who really stand out from the rest as being cream of the crop. Then ask yourself: what do they do?

Being able to identify the members of your team that go above and beyond offers a few benefits. First, it helps you translate their greatness to your customers and other vendors. When others realize how wonderful your team is, and why, they become extra excited to work with you.

Identifying the actions that took them to the top of your list may also spark some ideas on how to improve yourself. Just like I borrowed the donut idea from builders, you may come across a vendor's strategy that you can use to help promote your real estate business even more.

Don't forget to appreciate your team for the superstars they are. Take the time to thank them when they go above the call of duty. Offer your gratitude for the way they always take care of you.

When you make your team feel appreciated, they are more willing to continue to do the things that you enjoy. The mere fact that you tell them how much it means to you makes them want to do more. It inspires them to keep up the good work so they remain one of your superstars.

Firing Customers

Have you ever considered the fact that you don't have to work with every single customer?

No, we're not talking about Fair Housing discrimination. But sometimes you just don't always click well with your customers. In cases like this, it is okay to fire them, especially if they're being unreasonable, out of control, or putting you in a liable situation that could result in either violation of law or a legal dispute.

Firing customers can come in many different forms. That said, I do encourage you to always make it the customer's decision to leave and work with someone else. How? By giving them that opportunity and opening the door.

When you have a customer that you're not clicking with—for whatever reason—giving them the opportunity to work with someone else might be the best thing for everybody involved.

I had customers who came for an event in my area centered around motorcycles. Mind you, I know nothing about motorcycles. I've never owned one and I probably never will. So, the whole time I'm showing the property to these buyers, they're looking at motorcycles and talking about all the places to go and ride.

This is when I realized that I had absolutely nothing in common with these people. As a result, I was having an extremely hard time connecting, building rapport, and establishing a relationship.

However, I also knew that Dave from my office rode motorcycles and knows a lot about them. So, I asked my customers if I could refer them over to Dave because they might work better together, and they have a lot more in common.

They were willing to make the transfer and I got a referral fee out of the deal. That's the absolute best way to fire a customer. Not by saying, "I can't work with you, so you're out of here!" but by connecting them with someone who can work with them better, have a better outcome, and still make money off of it.

The other good thing about taking this approach is that it frees up your time to go work with customers that you do click with and can more easily make a sale or transaction.

Unfortunately, sometimes we have to fire customers for other reasons. They are unrealistic, mean, unprofessional, or putting us in a bad situation.

Do not ever be afraid to fire a customer. For some crazy reason, being willing to go through this process actually makes them respect you more. It says that you're willing to stand up to them and take responsibility for your business, even if it means walking away from the transaction.

Chapter Recap

- No matter how good you are, you can't do everything yourself. Make a list of the tasks you can delegate to others, especially if you can do it at less than you make per hour.
- Take some time to learn more about your personality so you gain a better understanding of who you are and how you interact with others. Use this to help you identify the areas where you may need more help.
- Set up a team of vendors you can trust with your transactions. Identify the superstars and let them know you appreciate what they do.
- Fire customers if you need to. If possible, do it in a way that connects them with another real estate agent so they walk away willingly.

Chapter 7
Listings

"Don't bring your need to the marketplace; bring your skill."
Jim Rohn, Entrepreneur, Author & Motivational Speaker

Canned Presentation

You finally have an appointment with a seller. You're super excited to have the potential of viewing their home and listing it for sale. So, what do you talk to them about? What do you show them? Do you have a canned presentation?

I call this a canned presentation because you show every single seller the same thing. Sure, you're going to tailor it from property to property but, overall, you should have similar information that you share with every seller. This includes:

- how you're going to market their property
- the websites you're going to showcase their home on
- installing a sign in their yard
- the market share that your company has
- how you and your team (including your vendor team) can assist them
- the actual process of selling the property

Your canned presentation should walk them all the way from the beginning to the end of the process. It should start with your plans for marketing the property, and move on to negotiations, appraisals, inspections, and getting their property sold. It ends with their money being transferred directly to them.

All these things answer questions that sellers may not even realize they need to ask.

Your canned presentation is typically going to be the first thing that you go over with your seller. Again, you sit down and show every single seller your presentation which includes this information.

Use lots of pictures as people are visual learners. Show them how their property is going to look on the MLS. Let them see the sign that will be in their front yard and get them to visualize how you will sell their property and get it sold.

Always use presumptive terms in your canned presentation. Tell them that you *will* sell their house versus that you *can* sell their house. Talk about how they *will* hire you and that you *will* accomplish the goal.

Having this same listing presentation showcases you, your company, and the marketing overall. It's really important that the seller understand these things. That they know what your communication will be and what's expected.

Sellers complain constantly that once a real estate agent lists their house for sale and leaves the listing appointment, they don't hear from them for a long time. Set yourself apart by committing to contact your seller on a regular basis, whether it's once a week or once every other week. Don't wait more than every two weeks to call them, even if you have no new information.

I commit to call my sellers every Monday. I will provide them feedback from any showings in the past week or remind them we haven't had any showings. They know I will call them every week, so they feel I live up to my promised word, and in addition, I get to remind them if there's no showings week after week, maybe it's time to discuss a price adjustment.

Once you go through your canned presentation, you can shift into your CMA and more customized information about their particular property.

Marketing the Product Online

In today's world, there are so many options and ways to market a listing for sale. We have technology and we have lots of opportunities to market the property all over the internet.

If you don't know where your properties are being marketed online, take a current listing that is for sale with yourself or your company and Google the address. You will be amazed at the websites that it comes up with. Websites you've probably never even heard of. Don't just stop at page 1 of Google, go deeper.

Sure, you'll get the most common ones like Realtor.com, Zillow, and Trulia, but you have no idea how many other websites are out there. There are literally hundreds that you're marketing properties on, so make sure you're communicating all of those places to your seller. I love to do that after I'm done listing the property for sale at the listing presentation.

Once I've explained the next steps, that we're going to place a sign in their yard and get professional pictures taken and so on, I tell them that I know they're excited about seeing their home on the internet and seeing the marketing that I'm going to do. I also reinforce that I really need a good week to get all their marketing stuff together.

After listing the property in the multiple listing service, I immediately set up a Google Alert to notify me in seven days for the property address. So, I receive an email in a week that shows me all the places the property is advertised. I then forward that email to the seller so that they can see all those places. There are usually around 100, if not more.

Now, this also includes international listings, so make sure you touch on the fact that you provide international marketing efforts as well. This might be done for you automatically through the IDX system if you are an MLS member.

There are plenty of additional ways to market the property, other than online. You can put fliers on the front yard sign and keep refilling them. This is kind of old school, but it still might be a viable option in your market.

You can have a rider sign (a smaller sign that accompanies the larger real estate sign) that has geocaching. This enables buyers to text a certain number, or it pops up on their phone when they're in the area and obtains the information about the house.

You can create a website solely for the property address. Alternatively, give it a dedicated page on your company's website. Send "Just Listed!" postcards to all area addresses, or you can only send them to the target market.

The list goes on and on when it comes to marketing properties. There are tons of ways you can do this. Just make sure you stay up with trends, so you provide the information potential buyers need in a way they prefer.

Speak to your brokerage company to find out what they offer as far as marketing. Then try to think of the many ways you can market your properties outside of these normal options. Be creative and see what you can come up with. Your customers will appreciate your additional efforts while setting you apart from other real estate professionals in your area.

Broker's Open Houses

There are a few different types of open houses. The first we will discuss is a broker's open house. This is basically where we open up the house to other real estate professionals in the area, other brokers and brokerages, and invite them into our property. How do you get them there? Bribe them with free food.

Set one specific day of the week and do a progressive lunch. Offer a salad at one house, the main course at another, and the desert at another. This will get brokers and brokerages to go to all three houses.

The idea behind doing this—which does cost some money—is that if I can attract 20 real estate professionals into my property and all 20 are working with 10 buyers each, I've just exposed that property to 200 potential buyers. But I do have a couple of rules of thumb.

When it comes to broker open houses, first, you must serve good food. If you do not serve good food, if you're somewhat chintzy, these people won't go to your next open house.

I don't mean you have to fully cater the 5-star meal, but you've got to make sure you have good quality food, and that you have enough of it. I've literally walked away from a broker's open house still hungry, even though I'd just spent three hours of my life there, then had to go buy myself lunch. Do not do this to your open house attendees.

Also, a broker's open house should include no more than three houses. I've been invited to progressive open houses involving six or seven homes. This takes all day and I don't have the time. It's too much. Promise me you will never do more than three houses.

My other rule of thumb is to only invite real estate professionals working with other companies. So, if I work for ABC Realty, I'm going to invite XYZ Realty. I want my people to come and support me, but I also want those company's agents to come and support them, which also brings them into my house. My coworkers already know about this listing. I need to expose it to other companies and pull those people in.

The other rule of thumb is that all the homes must be close to each other. You can't have people driving from downtown to Timbuktu. It's too much. Ideally, they should be in the same neighborhood or the same area, providing a much quicker process.

When these real estate professionals come into the property, we want to make sure that they actually see the property. I walked in behind a couple of people one day and they made a beeline to the kitchen, got their meatball sub, chitchatted for a few minutes with the listing agent, then walked back out the front door. That's when one of them turned to the other and said, "Wow! I didn't even realize there's a second floor. Did you go upstairs?"

"No," the other responded. "We don't have time. Come on, we've got to get to the next house."

What's the point of serving lunch if they're not even going to come in and look at the property and give you decent feedback, right? You've just wasted your time and money.

To encourage real estate professionals to take the complete tour, I also offer a feedback form. (You can download a free copy of this form from my website at https://CynthiaDeLuca.com/product/open-house-feedback-form/.) It asks three basic questions.

The first is: what do you think about the exterior of the property? Then I have three spots where they can circle whether it meets their expectations, exceeds their expectations, or is below their expectations. I also provide three or four blank lines where they can add their own comments.

The second question is: what do you think about the interior of the property? Again, they can circle whether it meets expectations, exceeds expectations, or is below expectations and have a few blank lines where they can put a comment in.

The last question is: what do you think about the price? Do you feel that it is at market value, above market value, or below market value?

I do not ask for their name or company name. I don't want any of that. I don't care. I only want them to be truthful with me.

I believe that you should always have somebody with you at your open houses, including your broker's opens. This could be a lender, a sponsor, a coworker, or a spouse.

Have them in the kitchen serving the food while you're at the front door with clipboards holding the meal ticket (feedback form), along with printouts of the MLS information so they can see the information about the house.

I hand the clipboard and ticket to them when they walk in and say, "Hey, walk around the house, check it out. Fill this out, bring your meal ticket to the kitchen and turn it in and you can get your meatball sub."

After the broker's open house, I take all of the feedback forms, scan, and email them to my seller. Why?

Have you ever told sellers to paint the wall because it is all scuffed up, yet they don't think it is a big deal? When they get 17 out of 19 feedback forms that all say, "You should paint that wall," you've made your point.

The feedback forms can also be enormously powerful for getting price adjustments and getting rid of smells. I've had suggestions put on these feedback forms that I never even thought of. So, use the opportunity to get the feedback forms and share them with your seller to inspire them to fix whatever it is before moving forward.

I don't have broker's opens on every property, just the ones that are giving me a little bit of trouble. Some properties you put on the market are going to sell right away. They're in good shape. So, I don't promise the seller initially that I'm going to do a broker's open.

If you do decide to have a broker's open, think about what time of day works best. In my mind, the majority of these are held at lunchtime, but you don't have to do that.

For instance, I've held a breakfast broker's open. I couldn't find anybody else that was willing to do it with me, so I held it by myself. I had the best turnout and literally had to push people out the door when it ended. I served mimosas and a breakfast casserole.

What I found was, from 8:30 to 10:30, real estate professionals aren't really doing much. You're not showing houses that early. Typically, you're either catching up at the office or whatnot. So, they would stop by and had plenty of time to chit chat with each other because they didn't have to run off and show a property or do anything.

Admittedly, not all my broker open houses have been successful. It can be hit or miss. Of course, when it rains, is cold outside, or the weather is gloomy, you may not get many attendees.

VIP Broker's Open

Sometimes you have a higher-priced property that is not necessarily going to sell super quick. This takes a certain group of buyers, ones with higher price ranges, to get these properties sold. In these cases, I have found that a VIP broker's open is very successful.

Let's say that you have a luxury property for sale, so you want to attract people with the ability to sell that property. The first thing I'm going to do is look up other properties in the area and price range that could share the expense of the VIP broker's open. Then I go into the MLS and search for agents who have sold a property in this price range in the past year.

Next, I put together custom invitations to a private event that is by invitation only and rent a limo bus. Not the kind that you have to duck to get into, but one that has the steps that go up with a little kitchenette area and seats down both sides. Typically these are more of a small bus style, versus a stretched car.

From there, we follow up with phone calls to ensure that they received the invitation *and* to make sure they understand that they cannot bring a guest. This event is just for them and we include everything for the day that they need. They just need to give us a day.

On the day of the VIP broker's open, we usually meet at one specific location, like an office parking lot, where we can leave our vehicles. We tell them to be there by 8:30 am even though the limo leaves at nine. This gives a little bit of time for people to meet and greet. Sometimes agents that are attending don't know each other or they've only seen the other agent's name but have never personally met.

When boarding the limo bus, we give them a bag breakfast which includes an individually wrapped muffin, a banana, an apple, and an orange. On the bus, there's orange juice and champagne. We do serve alcohol because they're not driving, and you can get a one-day insurance policy rider for this added to your general liability policy. Once everyone has arrived, we take off. This includes any sponsors.

We try to get as many sponsors for our VIP events as possible. Sometimes they will sponsor a certain segment, so they might get on and ride with us part of the time. There is a microphone and speaker system in those bus limos, so they can talk about who they are and what they do.

These houses are luxury, so we spend more time there, but we don't do more than six in a day. Usually, it's five. The only exception might be if you have multiple high-end condos in the same complex. Then, you may want to do more.

When we arrive at the property, there's always someone there with the house open and ready to go so we're not fidgeting with lockboxes or wasting time trying to get in the doors and open up windows. As agents unload off the bus, we tell them we will be leaving at 10:15 and to make sure they are back by then. In other words, we give them a time to return to the bus.

As a group, we go inside where the listing agent is to talk about the property, pass out information, and allow the attendees to go and look around. This agent also reminds them of what time they need to be back on the bus.

Since it is a luxury listing, there is likely plenty of room to roam. This also enables the agents enough time space to make and return confidential phone calls before returning to the bus to go to the next property.

We always do a sit-down, family-style lunch, so we have it catered by a local restaurant, usually Italian food. This allows for rapport building between the agents and they love this. They get to talk about the challenges of real estate, marketing, or whatever they'd like.

Also, while we're at lunch, someone goes into the limousine, removes all of the leftover breakfast goodies, and replaces them with an afternoon snack. They stock up on sodas, granola bars, and items like that because I'm a big believer that food is love. That is why cruise ships stuff you to the max with buffet lines and all you can eat. Plus, we never want them to feel like they need to leave to get the things they need. We have a wide variety of sodas, drinks, and snacks for them.

After lunch, we move on to the next house. At the last house of the tour, we always end with six margarita machines. Yes, six. People are fascinated by these, they love them. The reason why I have so many is that we might do a virgin pina colada in one and we might do a strawberry daiquiri with alcohol in a different machine (albeit somewhat light on the alcohol).

You can buy an alcohol policy, as mentioned previously, adding it to your general liability insurance for one day. It's usually a couple of hundred bucks.

We do this at the last house as a thank you for spending the day with us. Then we get back on the bus and arrive back at our parked cars before the promised time. We typically tell them 4:30 but always make sure we're back before then.

The very first year we did this, we secured enough sponsors to pay for the entire event. In the second year, we actually made a little bit of money. It wasn't much, somewhere around $200, but we still ended up ahead.

I've only had one year where it did cost us a little (like $150), where we didn't break even. Other than that, it's always been easy to get sponsors because they want to get in front of luxury agents and other companies involved in big-dollar real estate transfers.

You could also do this type of event with a mixture of different agents that all agree to chip in or try to get sponsorships. Typically, before the week is over, they'll reach out with a thank you note. I even had people sell a deal in the limousine. It wasn't our luxury listing, but that's okay. They struck a deal on a property, all because of our VIP Broker’s Open bringing them together.

Others have been able to strike additional deals, so they're constantly asking when the next VIP Broker's open house is going to be. "Can we go on your waiting list?" they'll ask. "We want to be invited next year!"

Public Open Houses

In a public open house, we're inviting everybody to come in. I would recommend that you always put the open house in your MLS system at least one week in advance because this shares it on Realtor.com and other websites.

Hopefully, we get some buyers to come, but you'll also get a lot of nosy neighbors. To deal with this non-buying traffic, I schedule a VIP hour, one hour before the general open house.

So, let's say my open house is between noon and two o'clock. I will hold a VIP hour from 11 to 12 for the neighborhood or community to come in and look around. You can notify them by knocking on their doors or mailing postcards. Suddenly, it becomes a community social hour. All the nosy neighbors come and chit chat with their other neighbors.

This may seem like a waste of time, but there are a couple of things I try to get from nosy neighbors when they are there. For instance, I try to get a good feel for where they live.

Normally, you want to have a sign-in sheet at an open house. But when it's the nosy neighbors coming for that specific hour, I know why they're there. I know the intention. And I know what I want to do. So, I don't always force them to sign in.

Instead, I have a conversation with them and figure out where to begin. "Which house do you live in? Oh, you're the third one down on the other side of the street?" I make a mental note of that, writing it down somewhere after the VIP hour. (I'm going to do a follow up with that and I'll tell you what that is in a minute.) So, they come in, look around, and chat with their other neighbors, just catching up on things.

Noon rolls around and it's time for your regular open house. Do you kick the neighbors out? Not necessarily.

Have you ever had people drive by at the beginning of your open house real slow and not stop? Having the neighbors there when this occurs contributes to what I call *the restaurant factor*.

We've already talked about this briefly, but this involves choosing a busy restaurant over one that is empty because we convince ourselves that the food must be better at the one that is packed. In other words, *activity breeds activity*.

So now someone drives by at 12 o'clock and says, “Wow! There are four cars there and that open house just started two minutes ago. Stop the car. We're going into this one!”

Once they come in and are looking around, their amazement continues. “Oh my gosh! All of these people are here for this open house? This must be *the* house.” By having a lot of people there, you’re creating that sense of urgency.

Before we move on, let me back up and tell you about the nosy neighbor first before I forget. Why do you think nosy neighbors come to the open house? Maybe they want to sell in the future. Or, in many cases, they are interested in learning what *their* house is worth.

Everyone always wants to know how much their house is worth. So, when I’m back in the office on Monday, I spend an hour doing surprise CMAs for the people that stopped by.

In a sealed envelope, I put a cover letter with the CMA valuation of their house and leave it on their front doorstep as part of the *wow* factor. In the cover letter, it says, "Thanks so much for stopping by my open house! I appreciate the time you took to chat with me. I thought you might be interested in what your home was valued at currently."

I also put something in there that says that all of the information was pulled from public records. I encourage them to call me and make an appointment if they would like a more detailed valuation of their property. It triggers that call to action, especially if they are interested in selling.

It's not very often that they take me up on this offer. Most of the time, they're just nosy neighbors. But I still want to deliver the *wow* factor. I want to impress them with the fact that I took the time to do the CMA, even though they didn't ask for it.

Again, they may not be interested in selling, but they may know someone who is. This keeps me at the forefront of their mind. I also add them to my database, so they get my newsletter four times a year. Okay, back to the public open house.

Now you've got buyers that walk in and they're interested. I give each one a folder. One side contains all the information about the property. This includes printed out pictures, as well as the details listed in the MLS.

Before the open house, I also go in and draw a map in the MLS of the surrounding area, find other active listings in the area, and print out a report to put on that side of the folder. In this report, it prints out one picture and basic property details. I put a cover letter with it explaining I can help with any home they find and that's it.

Sometimes one of these other properties will pique a buyer's interest. If this occurs, I never leave an open house to show that property. I think that shows disrespect to the seller. Instead, I tell them that I can meet them right after the open house. I try to be very respectful of people and think that the buyers appreciate it as well.

One time, I had a seller walk up, open the folder, and ask why I was giving buyers all these other properties. My response is that buyers want to know the market. They want to see the properties they have access to. It also shows them that the house the seller is selling is priced appropriately, increasing the likelihood that they will move forward and make an offer. That satisfied the seller.

On the other side of the folder is information about me. I have my business card and a personal brochure that provides a little bit more insight into me personally. I share what my interests are, and my unique value proposition is, or what makes me different and why people should hire me.

I also include my resume. When you're in an open house and a buyer walks in, you are trying to be hired. So, it's just kind of saying, "Here are my qualifications for getting hired."

Public open house attendees are also given a feedback form, just like in my broker's opens. I don't require them to fill it out but have found that buyers like to be involved and might pick it up on their own and complete it.

On public open houses, I place a sign on the outside of the front door that says that you must show a photo ID to enter. This helps with safety and liability. If people don't want to provide personal information due to not wanting to be contacted for follow-up, I include a box that they can check on the sign-in form.

Door Knocking

I enjoy door knocking when I have the time. You typically have more time at the beginning of your career, and not a lot of money. Then as you start getting busy, you must make that shift to where when you have less time and spend more money on things to make up for that difference.

But it's more about the *wow* factor. It's getting the person on the other side of the door to think, "Man! If that real estate professional is willing to come out and knock from door to door, they're probably going to do whatever it takes to get my house sold. And if I refer them to a neighbor or friend, they're probably going to do whatever it takes to get their house sold."

Before you go, pay attention to whether the community says "no solicitation." Unfortunately, people still solicit them, but we don't want to be that person.

If all is clear, put on a good pair of shoes and walk door to door. I always do this with a partner, though we each take opposite sides of the street so we can hit more houses and still keep an eye on each other. I also never go inside the house, again, for safety's sake.

If I knock on the door and someone answers, I say, "Hey, I'm just in the neighborhood. I want to let you know that I can help if you ever need a real estate agent." I hand them a business card and go to the next house.

If no one answers—whether because they aren't home or aren't willing to answer the door to a stranger—I leave a door hanger that says, "Sorry, we missed you." Each has a slot where I can insert my business card.

What's your first thought when you see a hanger like this? It's usually something along the lines of, "Why were you here?" This leads them to call me and find out. Once they've called, I now have permission to follow up with them.

When they contact me, I'll say, "No worries. Listen, I was out in the neighborhood to meet some of your neighbors today. I just wanted to let you know that I'm searching for new customers. So, if you ever have a need for anything in real estate, I'd be glad to help. If you want to know the value of your property, I could also do a free CMA."

If they want a CMA, put them into your CRM database so you can keep following up with them. Eventually, they will get to know you and hopefully either use you or refer you to others.

Door knocking is great if you don't have a lot of money but do have some time. It's also good if you have money but want to spend less when marketing your listings.

Chapter Recap

- Develop a canned presentation to ensure that every seller receives the same type of information about their property and how you do business.
- There are several different ways to market your properties. Follow the most traditional but also don't be afraid to think outside the box.
- Hold broker's open houses on listings that aren't selling quickly, increasing the number of agents interested in making the sale.
- For certain types of properties, such as luxury properties, VIP broker's open houses may be worth the investment, especially when sponsors pay for some or all the cost.
- Conducting a successful public open house involves working with neighbors, adding more names to your database.
- Door knocking shows that you're willing to go the extra mile with your listings. Just be safe when you do it.

Chapter 8
Buyers

"Nobody likes to be sold, but everyone likes to buy."

Dr. Earl Taylor, Leadership and Sales Trainer

Pre-Qualification vs Pre-Approval

Recently I saw a post in a Facebook group for real estate professionals that asked why it was important to prequalify a buyer before showing them a property. That poor person got blasted, why?

Prequalifying a buyer tells you whether they can afford the property that has piqued their interest. It tells you what range to look in so you're not wasting your time or theirs showing them homes they can't afford.

Sometimes buyers will do some of their own investigation, such as reviewing an amortization schedule to figure out their payment and whether they're comfortable with it. However, what they don't realize is that this payment doesn't include their taxes, insurance, or association fees. Helping them understand this keeps them from setting unrealistic expectations.

I'm also a big believer in buyers and sellers having buy-in during the process. Buy-in means they're investing time and energy for the transaction as well. I am not going to be the only one spinning my wheels because it's too easy for them to change their mind. I want them to prove to me that they're willing to do what it takes to move forward, to show that they're interested enough to go through the pre-qualification or pre-approval process. What's the difference between the two?

With pre-qualification, the buyer literally does nothing, except for maybe answering some questions on the phone about how much they make, what other debt they have, and their credit score.

Speaking of credit score, some buyers confuse "advantage" scores as being the same thing as a FICO score. However, companies like Credit Karma and CreditWise enable you to boost this score, but it's not the same thing as getting a higher credit rating.

A true FICO-based credit rating can only be established by a lender verifying that there is money in the bank and that you earn a specific amount of income. This is part of the pre-approval process and requires that the buyer supply the required information. They must take some form of action, giving them some buy-in.

Unfortunately, not all lenders are willing to go through the pre-approval process. So, I encourage you to call up *your* lenders, take them to lunch, pick their brains, and let them tell you what's going on in the financing world right now. Ask them if they're willing to <u>fully</u> approve your buyer before they find a house.

To fully approve (not pre-approve) they must send it through underwriting. But you know that when you have a fully approved buyer, the only thing left to do is find a house and close. After the appraisal, termite inspection, and whatever else is required, of course. So fully approved is even better.

In short, the pre-qualification process helps educate buyers, so they understand how much money they'll need to close, what they're comfortable with paying, and so on. The pre-approval process ensures that they have the financial means to follow through with the transaction while also forcing them to buy-in to the process by supplying all the necessary documentation.

Cash Transactions

What if you have a buyer who says that they are paying cash? It may seem unlikely, but 12% of all transactions in my market are cash transactions, and your MLS statistics can tell you about your market.

So, when talking to a new buyer, I will ask, "Are you one of the fortunate 12% of buyers in today's market that can pay with cash, or do you want to speak with a lender about obtaining financing?" The reason I say it this way is if ask outright whether they need financing, you might as well say, "Are you a deadbeat who doesn't have the money?"

That's the way I feel like it's coming across, so I want to be very sensitive about that. Instead, by saying it the way I do, I'm essentially telling them, "Look, it's okay because only 12% of buyers in my market pay cash."

If they do say that they're paying cash, I want to get proof of funds before they ever see a property. There's a couple of ways you can do this.

One is to request a copy of their bank statement or investment account. The problem with this is that if they show proof of funds that they have $800,000 in their bank, yet they're only buying a $300,000 house, the seller won't want to negotiate because they will know that your buyer can pay more.

To get around this, a lot of times, they'll get a letter from the bank that says they have enough funds to pay at least $300,000 or whatever the price range for the property. Sadly, there's a lot of fraud with these proofs.

I don't trust anyone, so I call the bank that issued the letter and ask them to verify whether the letter is real or fraudulent. This begins by asking about the person who signed the letter to ensure that they are an employee.

I did this once and the person on the phone told me that the name on the letter was the CEO. "Of the branch?" I asked. No, of the entire nationwide bank. Immediately I knew it was fake.

Do the same thing with proof of funds. Call the lender if they came already pre-approved and verify. "Hey, Joe just came in and wants to buy a house. I'm going to help him with this, and he told me he was already pre-qualified through you. I do have your letter here. So, can you just tell me a little bit about the loan? Is it going to be VA, conventional, or FHA? How much do they expect to put down, so I know how to structure the offer?"

One time, a lender said, "Can you send me that letter?" I scanned it and sent it to him, and he called me back to say that the buyers had whited out his date. He had not talked to them in over six months, but they didn't want to have to keep going back and updating information, so they just whited out the date and figured nobody would ask.

People will do weird things to get in the door of a property. Make sure you prequalify them. Ask whether they'll be paying cash or are in need of a loan, and if they need a loan, get them pre-approved.

If they're getting financing but putting down a large deposit, you might want to get proof of funds for that deposit. Again, this keeps you from wasting your time because they don't have the money to proceed.

Canned Presentation Part 2

Just as you want to have a canned presentation for sellers, you also should have one for buyers. This is a presentation that you provide each buyer you work with. It includes the same type of information every time, even though the individual data will change based on the property involved.

Information to include in a canned presentation directed toward buyers includes:

- Who you are and what sets you apart from other real estate agents
- Your process when working with buyers
- All your contact information so they can get in touch with you easily
- Information on the property or properties of interest to them
- Contact information for lenders you recommend when getting pre-approved
- A cheat sheet to help them better understand common real estate terms

Establishing a process where each buyer receives the same information from you ensures that you don't forget to provide an important piece of data. It also enables you to master your canned presentation over time. It becomes natural to you because you've been through the process so many times.

If you're working with a buyer who is a referral, it's likely that the person who recommended you gave them some idea of what to expect. A canned presentation helps you deliver on that expectation. It also makes it easier for them to refer you because they know that you have the same high level of service each and every time.

Practice your buyer presentation until you know it like the back of your hand. When you can deliver information fluently, it sets your buyer at ease. They develop a level of trust in you, reinforcing that they made the right decision by choosing you as their agent.

Tell Me About a Day in Your Life…

Of course, you can't provide a property buyer unbeatable service if you don't know anything about them. That's like trying to sell someone a music album without first knowing whether they prefer pop, rock, R&B, country, or rap. You're not going to get very far.

There are a ton of ways you can gain a better understanding of your buyer. Most involve asking numerous questions to determine what they like, what they don't like, and more. If you're not careful, they can begin to feel like they're being interrogated, which isn't at all good when you're trying to affect a sale.

Instead, I have found that you can find out a ton of information by asking buyers one simple question: *"Tell me what a day in your life looks like."*

The great thing about taking this approach is that it is completely open-ended. You're giving them the floor to tell you whatever it is they feel is important for you to know. And they're doing it in a way that feels less intrusive or interrogatory.

Plus, they may share information that they didn't think was relevant to buying a home but could actually impact the type of property they'd be most happy with.

For example, if the client tells you that they start their day by sitting and reading the paper or scanning their tablet for news, this tells you that a home with a sitting room would offer this buyer some benefits. Conversely, if they start their day by working out, a property with an exercise room would likely be more appealing.

If their day involves attending their children's sporting events, properties in close proximity to the school or sporting fields could be more attractive. If they like to stop at fast food restaurants on their way home, finding homes with these types of establishments in the vicinity can help make the sale.

In today's world, people are constantly looking for ways to make their life easier. By having a buyer tell you about their typical day, you are able to identify where their pain points exist. Find a way to overcome these and your properties will climb to the top of their list.

Maybe they indicate that struggle with having such a long commute. Locating properties that can reduce the amount of time spent going to and from work is a good selling point to focus upon. You can get a lot of information simply by listening to them talk about their normal day.

If you want more information, follow up by asking them if they could change anything about their day, what would it be. Their answer may not be able to be solved by buying a property. But if it does, knowing this helps you find a home that makes their lives better, happier, or more fulfilled. All because you took the time to listen.

Naming the House

A minor, yet effective sales tactic that is known for making a property more appealing is to give it a name. Most any television show that revolves around buying properties already knows that this is one way to make a particular house more appealing.

Labeling a listing as "The Bungalow" or "The Retreat" creates an image in the buyer's mind. Better yet, it also evokes a pleasurable feeling. They begin to connect that property with positive emotions, strengthening their desire to want to own it.

Admittedly, coming up with names for all your houses isn't always easy. You may find yourself cycling through the same descriptors over and over again.

To avoid this, imagine that you had to sell the house but could only use one- or two-word descriptors. Which descriptors would you use to accurately portray the value the home offers?

If you struggle with this, enlist the help of your co-workers. Ask them what they think of when looking at the property. Which words come to mind?

Another option is to wait until you've shown the listing a few times. Ask potential buyers what they think after viewing the property. They might offer up some new words that paint the perfect image, even if it wasn't the right home for them.

Some homes come already named. For instance, if a home is the biggest one on the street, the neighbors may refer to it as "The Mansion." This provides a glimpse of the fact that they'll own the largest property on the block.

Or maybe neighbors call it the "Old Schoolhouse." Including this in your listing is a great way to share the home's history with the buyer. It evokes some curiosity as they wonder how that property got its name.

Oftentimes, properties receive their names based on the style of the home, such as "The Cottage" or "The Nook." You can also name a home based on its location by incorporating "Woodlands" or "Hillcrest" in the name.

If the area around the home is known for its vegetation, you can use this in the name as well. "The Hollies" and "Honeysuckle" are both examples of naming a property by flowers and plants in the area.

Chapter Recap

- Pre-qualifying buyers is different than getting them pre-approved. Ideally, you want to pre-approve your buyers through a lender so you don't waste time trying to sell them a home they can't afford. Pre-approval also helps them buy into the process so they are more likely to complete the transaction.
- Ask your buyers whether they will be paying with cash or credit in a way that makes them feel okay if financing must be obtained.
- Develop a canned presentation for buyers to ensure that each one gets the same level of service every time.
- One of the best ways to learn the type of property that is best for a buyer is to ask them to tell you what a day in their life looks like.
- Naming your properties makes them more appealing because, in addition to evoking a good image, they also evoke a positive emotion.

Chapter 9
Keep In Touch

"Don't ignore the effort of a person who tries to keep in touch, it's not all the time someone cares."
Unknown Author

Caring

I get a common question a lot as I'm speaking about the importance of keeping in touch. People ask me, when is it too much keeping in touch? In other words, they don't want to overly bother the person. Well, I say if you do it right, they will look forward to your connections. This starts with caring. When you genuinely care for your customers, their well-being, their families, their careers, and more, they can see you are not in the relationship for the sale. Transactional selling is so last decade. Relationship selling is the here and now. People want to know you care about them. If they do not feel you care, you might as well be a used car salesperson, because that's what you are.

So how do you care? This starts by promising yourself that everything you send your database will not just be about you, but about how it can help the customer. Let's look at some examples of things we can use to keep in touch with our database:

- Current market stats
- Free home valuations
- E-newsletter with valuable information
- Updates on events happening in your local area
- A customer appreciation event once a year

- A small token of appreciation, or a gift once or twice a year.
- Holiday cards
- Birthday cards
- Home purchase anniversary cards
- Personalized handwritten note card
- A phone call to check-in
- Just sold announcements every time you have a sale (more on this to come)
- Press releases of awards you win or designations you earn
- Donut visit (remember Chapter 5?)
- A pie for the holidays
- A birthday cake delivered

What's important to remember, in everything you use to connect with your database, is that it's about *them*, not you. Let me give you some examples.

Congratulations, you've earned a designation. Let's say you took the Accredited Buyer's Representative (ABR) designation course and acquired the designation, and you want to tell your database all about it. You could send them something like this:

Congratulations are in order. I have just achieved my ABR designation. I had to endure multiple days of classroom education so I could learn how to make buyers more accountable, have them sign a contract binding them to work with me, and ensure I get paid when the transaction closes. This means I'll be more comfortable working with buyers in the future.

That doesn't sound very good to me. In other words, if I'm your customer, why in the heck do I care about all that? Sounds like you're patting yourself on the back, and it doesn't improve your client's life or real estate experience any.

Now, let's change it up a bit.

Congratulations are in order. In my never-ending journey to be a better REALTOR® for you, I have just earned my ABR designation. ABR stands for "Accredited Buyer Representative". To receive my ABR, I had to complete extensive training regarding the buying aspect of the real estate transaction.

Some of the things I learned include all the benefits buyers receive when hiring a REALTOR®, negotiation strategies, alternative ways to find that perfect property, offer and counter-offer strategies, updates on the financing and appraisal processes and so much more.

Along with how to serve my customers better, I also learned how to keep myself out of trouble. These topics included the Fair Housing Laws and Professional Standards.

I hope this education will help me serve my customers better, both existing and future. To have my ABR designation is truly a prestigious accomplishment. When you deal with me, you can feel confident that I will be as professional and knowledgeable as possible. I look forward to putting this knowledge to work for you. Please call me if you are interested in buying or selling any property, or if you know someone who is.

See the difference? It's about them and how what you just did helps the buyer or seller. Always make sure what you craft or send out is about the client. They are priority number 1.

Another example might be a simple phone call or a handwritten note. You don't necessarily need to have a reason to contact them, just a simple "I was thinking about you and wanted to check in and see how you were." is good enough. Show them you care. You don't have to discuss real estate at all during the conversation. They should know from your other marketing efforts that you are a real estate professional. Now, once you check-in, they remember that you are *their* real estate professional.

By the way, if you have the ABR designation, GRI, SRS, PSA, or others, I have an announcement already crafted for you, ready to use. Visit my website at https://CynthiaDeLuca.com/ and download them from my shop.

One and done

I am always amazed when I am coaching a real estate professional to hear they have succumbed to the "one and done" mentality.

Let's say you sell a property in a neighborhood that you want to acquire more listings in. So you go to your favorite print shop, have them create a postcard that says you sold the property with a few details, and mail it to the entire surrounding area, costing you a pretty penny.

Then you wait. Crickets. You get no phone calls, no contacts, no nothing. None of those neighbors need to sell their house? Weird. Oh well, then you move on to the next listing, in a different neighborhood. You are successful in selling that and send out just sold postcards to that neighborhood and again, crickets.

This, my friends, is what I call the "one and done".

Let me back up here and explain that I graduated from college and worked in the advertising industry. From my days in marketing, we worked with some of the top companies around the world and the experiences were amazing.

No matter how big or smart we thought these companies were, they all had one similar thing in common when they came to us. They succumbed to the one and done mentality.

Whether it was placing a magazine ad in an international magazine or sending out a sample product in amazing packaging, they only budgeted to do it once. Once.

We had a rule of thumb in the advertising world: They need to see you every 10 days to convert to a customer.

Every 10 days is no small task. That means to accomplish this, you've got to mix it up. Maybe they receive your e-newsletter, then a couple of weeks later, they see your bus bench advertising alongside the road, then a couple of weeks later, they see your social media post, and so on. You get the idea. Be everywhere all the time so they begin to recognize you and remember you.

The problem with the one and done is you can't accomplish that. You send out the postcard once to the neighborhood, get no response, then move on to the next neighborhood.

My theory behind this is because they don't know you and they forget about you, just like that. They may also already have a relationship with a real estate professional that is doing a great job of consistently following up.

Either way, quit wasting your money on the one and done.

Your Massive Database

Truth be told, most of the items in the list a few pages ago of ways to keep in touch is reserved for your closest 100. You don't want to send a birthday cake to everyone in your massive database of 5,000 people. That just doesn't make sense. So most of those items are for your closest 100.

What you can do to keep in touch with your massive database is fairly simple. Send them an e-newsletter at least quarterly, if not monthly. Keep them engaged with the real estate market, whether it's good or bad news. Knowing what the real estate market is doing and where values are going is always a hot topic for anyone, and that information is so easy to access. Offer them ways to connect with you on a deeper level. For example, you might have a section where they can request an updated valuation (CMA) of their property, they just need to submit their info and request it and you will provide it within 3 business days, or something similar.

Again, most of the items, including the yearly valuation, will only be for your closest 100. It's easy to complete 100 CMA's in a year, but not 5,000. So give them the opportunity to engage further, which helps you discover that they might be ready or interested to pursue a real estate purchase or sale, and your follow up means with you!

Your Influential Database

Remember your influential database we discussed in chapter 4? Let's talk about what to send them and how to connect with them as influencers.

First, let me remind you these people are influencers, meaning they have influence over others. They might be high profile people in your area, business owners, the mayor, etc.

Be like-minded. People rub elbows with others who have similar interests, hobbies, friends, etc. Start by "hanging out" where these people hang out. That could be offline and that could be online. LinkedIn is a great place to start and make connections online. Offline, it might be joining the Chamber of Commerce for your area and getting involved. Being in the spotlight and letting them get to know you from a distance is always helpful.

Next, you want to start target marketing them. So, what do you send them? First, let's think about ways you can help them. Remember, always look through the eyes of the client and answer the question "Why should I get to know this real estate professional?"

If they have employees, remember the VIP program? You can reach out and offer your services to assist their employees in purchasing or selling a home. Now you come with benefits and they want to get to know you.

Another idea is to drip campaign them. This is done by sending them a letter or contact once every two weeks for a total of six contacts, then you follow up with personal contact such as a phone call or office visit. Your drip campaign can be something like this:

- Put my experience to work for your staff, for free!
- Your employees are my priority

- I am accepting new clients
- Let me introduce myself
- Real estate headaches? I can help.
- Tired of fishing in an ocean full of real estate professionals? (on fish themed paper-then explain why you are different)

These are just the headings and you can fill it in with valuable info that shows them why they should get to know you. So, the first letter for example would include info about how you only get paid once all parties are satisfied and closed. If you offer a cancellation policy or service guarantee, this is where I would mention that. Tell them what you offer that is above normal service, that *Wow* service we discussed.

Then a couple of weeks later, letter number 2 arrives. Remember, this not a one and done. Commit to this timeline and multiple contacts.

Now, for this, I prefer the good old-fashioned snail mail. I place the letters in a plain envelope and write "confidential" on the envelope. I do that in hopes that a secretary or receptionist won't open the letter and immediately trash it. I want it to get in the hands of the intended target.

Remember, after you've crafted your letters and mailed them, put it on your calendar to follow up in person or over the phone with them. Ask them to lunch to get to know them better and see how you can help them with their challenges. Build a relationship. And don't forget, you could always bring a box of donuts when you drop into their office.

Want a detailed plan of ways to keep in touch with the people in your database? Just go to my website, www.CynthiaDeLuca.com, and you can download a free follow up plan. For this item, make sure you use the coupon code *"Standout"*. That way you can download the items for free, just for you reading this book, my standout crowd.

Chapter Recap

- Show your buyers you care, not just about the transaction, but about them.
- Ensure your marketing materials are designed to help the buyer and seller, not just talk about you.
- Commit to never do a "one and done" marketing piece again.
- Differentiate what you will send to your massive database versus your influential database.
- Stick to a detailed plan to keep in touch.

Section 4

The Ballast Effect

Chapter 10

Balance

"You want to strike that happy medium: the balance of being able to find creative satisfaction in your profession, be able to afford a roof over your head, but still have the freedom to live a relatively normal life."

Chris Evans, American Actor

Scheduled Time

Have you ever had those days where you wake up and have certain things you want to get done, but the day just starts crazy? And you run around like a crazy chicken with its head cut off but, by the time the day is over, you realize that you actually didn't accomplish anything? Of course, we all have. One of the ways you can keep these days to a minimum is to follow a strict work schedule.

You can start each week with a long list of things you need to accomplish, but the problem is that time can easily get away from you. Before you know it, it's Friday afternoon and your to-do list is still as long as ever. A better way is to schedule time on your calendar to do the things you need to get done.

Consider all the things you must do to ensure a strong business and growing revenue. This regularly involves networking, marketing, and advertising yourself and your business. It is also important to schedule time to meet with potential buyers and sellers, show new listings, hold open houses, negotiate contracts, order title work, and the list goes on and on…and on.

To keep from being overwhelmed while creating a successful business, start at the beginning. Find buyers and sellers. Once you get a good string of clients and have a few successful transactions, strive to keep in touch with past customers. Regularly contact people in all your databases, but especially your most influential and closest 100. What does an effective work schedule look like?

Mondays tend to be a slower day for being out of the office and showing property, so I get done as much as I can while I'm in the office. Even on the other days, the mornings aren't usually super busy in real estate because showings don't typically start until 10 a.m. or later.

So, between 8:30 and 10, I do some marketing, update my website, etc. I also use this time to call my sellers and let them know what's going on with showings or to update my pending contracts to verify that title work has been ordered, the lender is up-to-date with what they need, and so on.

By scheduling these tasks, I am sure to allow myself enough time to take care of them and get them done. This also leaves me the rest of the day to meet with buyers and sellers without worrying about all of the other tasks on my to-do list. I know that they are scheduled as well and that they will be taken care of soon enough.

Of course, each of us has a different weekly schedule. Therefore, you need to adapt this to one that works for you. Essentially, you are just taking the tasks that you know must get done and scheduling them within your calendar, like an appointment.

What if something comes up during that time frame? To deal with this type of situation, I leave myself miscellaneous time. That way, if I have someone in town that wants to go out and look at properties on Monday morning—when I'm usually in the office—it's no problem. I'm definitely not going to turn away a buyer. I simply take the miscellaneous time that I had calendared later that week and schedule my other tasks then.

If I'm all caught up, awesome. That time becomes a bonus. You can go get a massage, enjoy a pedicure, get your frustrations out at the gym, or whatever you want or need to do. You are caught up so you can do these things guilt-free.

Scheduling your time is a wonderful way to take control of your real estate business, and your time. It ensures that you're doing the things that are necessary for your long-term success.

Hours of Business Operation

Real estate is not a 9-5 industry. Your schedule tends to revolve around the schedule of your buyers and sellers. This typically means that you're working when they're not.

That's why it's common to see open houses scheduled in the morning or early afternoon on weekends. Most of the rest of the world is off work, making it possible to visit your listing.

Evening appointments are also normal in real estate. When buyers and sellers are tied up during the day working their jobs, the only time they typically have available to tend to their personal matters is after work. This makes nighttime hours a must when buying or selling homes.

You can handle setting your hours of operation in a few different ways. The first is to dictate regular hours, such as 8 a.m. to 8 p.m. This provides your clients with a wide range of times to meet with you to list or view properties.

Another option is to set reduced hours with the notation that you are available at other times by appointment only. This still provides your customers flexibility without feeling like you must be always ready to get up and go during all your waking hours.

An example of this is to indicate that you are available from 9 a.m. to 7 p.m. but would be glad to schedule earlier or later appointments to better accommodate your clients.

You can also vary your schedule based on the times that are typically slower or busier. If you have noticed that you rarely get contacted before noon on Tuesdays, set your hours so you start a little later this day of the week. This allows you to either take the morning off so you can work later into the evening or you can use this time to catch up on other stuff.

The main thing to remember when it comes to setting your operations is to make sure your buyers and sellers know when you are available. If you don't answer the phone after 8 p.m., let them know. This way they aren't sitting there wondering why you won't take their call.

A good time to do this is during your canned presentations. Talk about your schedule and your policies regarding setting appointments outside of your dedicated hours of operation to all your buyers and sellers.

If you require 24 hours' notice when setting an off-time appointment, for example, make sure they understand this. If there is a specific day of the week you are not available, such as if your child has music lessons every Wednesday night and you need to take her and pick her up, tell them this too.

Giving the details about your schedule also gives you the opportunity to ask about their schedule.

Inquire about the hours they work and when they are typically free to handle the buying or selling of property. Knowing this in advance makes it easier to anticipate when they will likely need you to be available too.

State and NAR Conventions

Attending conventions is a great way to stay up to date on the latest and greatest in real estate. These events are also wonderful opportunities to network with others in the field, making important connections and sharing tricks of the trade.

Take time two to three times per year to look for state and national conventions. In the case of the latter, you can turn this learning and networking event into a vacation by going a few days early or staying a couple of days over.

One to keep your eye on is the National Association of Realtors® (NAR). They publish their annual meetings on their website at https://www.nar.realtor/events/nar-meetings-by-year. This agency offers conferences, legislative meetings, leadership summits, and trade expos. Each one is typically held in a different location across the U.S. This enables you to select the one that is most appealing to you.

If it is in a destination you want to explore more, take your family with you. Give them time to relax while you're learning more about the real estate industry, then set out to see the local sites once your day is done.

A few of the destinations for NAR conferences include Las Vegas, Nevada; Chicago, Illinois; Orlando, Florida; Washington, D.C.; Boston, Massachusetts; and Atlanta, Georgia. All these locations are a great place to vacation.

Real Estate Alert also offers links to a variety of conferences at https://www.realert.com/market/calendar.pl. These are organized by main events, events inside the U.S., and events outside the U.S. For each event listed, it identifies the location, dates, and organizer. You can also click on individual events to be directed to their website, so you can either learn more information or sign up to attend.

The World Academy of Science, Engineering, and Technology also offers a list of real estate conferences held around the world at https://waset.org/real-estate-conferences. These are broken down by year and include the location and date of the events. If you click on the conference title, you are directed to a page that provides more information, such as the venue, registration fees, conference photos, a flyer, and the program.

Signing up for these events as early as possible can sometimes save you money "early bird" registration fees are often reduced. This also gives you advanced notice of when you will not be available to meet with your clients.

If possible, have another agent fill in for you when you are gone. Direct your phone calls to them by changing your voicemail message to include that person's name and number. Tell your buyers and sellers in advance so they understand when you'll be away and how you plan to still tend to their needs during that time.

It cannot be stressed enough that communication is key when it comes to keeping your clients happy. As long as they know what to expect when it comes to the times you are available and the times you are not, they'll be more likely to work with you versus seeking a competitor.

Work-Life Balance

Since being involved in real estate typically means working non-traditional hours and long days, it can be hard to achieve a level of work-life balance. That said, being dedicated to the point where you have little to no home life can be harmful to your mental and physical health. Not to mention, that's not a very enjoyable way to live life.

Certainly, if you want to make money buying and selling real estate, you must be flexible with your time. Nighttime and weekend appointments are to be expected, sometimes on truly little notice.

But don't be afraid to also schedule a time that will be spent with family and friends. Actually, putting these "appointments" on your calendar serves as a great reminder that the people you love are just as important as having a career you love.

Along the same lines, just because your phone rings doesn't mean that you have to take the call immediately. If your child is in the middle of telling you about his day at school, let the call go to voicemail. You can call them back in a few minutes, enabling you to conduct your business while also showing your child that he or she is valued and loved.

When you are first starting out, it's a bit harder to find that work-life balance. You put in extra hours to grow your customer base, going above and beyond to show that you are a real estate professional who is worth working with.

Once you have a good customer base established, give yourself permission to ease up a bit. Aim to spend a little more time at home versus always being on the job.

If you go through periods where all you do is work, work, work, schedule a well-deserved vacation. Take the time to regularly recharge your battery so you don't get burnt out. Go far away and unplug from the real estate world.

It is great to be dedicated to your career and offer top-notch customer service to your customers, just don't do it at the expense of yourself. Give yourself regular periods of downtime to recoup and regroup. This offers benefits to you mentally, but also helps protect your physical health.

Achieving some level of work-life balance also keeps your stress levels lower. You don't feel so consumed with buying and selling property, to the point where you fret over every little thing. It ensures that you have enough joy in your life to keep you going, especially when times get tough.

No one is immune from facing hard times. Family members get sick, relationships fall apart, and homes need unforeseen repairs. If you have a work-life balance, these issues become easier to deal with. You have the mental and physical energy to handle them head on instead of being so worn out from working all of the time that you aren't able to cope with whatever lies ahead.

Set aside a few hours a week just for you. Get a massage, stay home and read a book, or catch up on your favorite shows. Don't feel guilty either because self-care is critical to also being successful in business.

Make a list of the places you want to vacation in the next five years. Aim to cross one of them off per year. Start planning your next vacation now. Decide where you're going to go, research accommodations, and begin getting it set up. The excitement you feel going through this process will spill over into your professional life and who doesn't like to work with a happy, energetic real estate agent?

Making yourself a priority isn't selfish, not even close. It simply ensures that you are at your best because you understand the value of downtime and of taking care of yourself.

If you're not accustomed to taking time off, it may feel strange at first. But chances are also good that, once you get over that feeling, you'll wonder what took you so long to schedule this time on your calendar.

Chapter Recap

- Schedule your time so you take care of important tasks such as marketing, updating your website, and contacting the people in your databases.
- Set your hours of operation in a way that makes the most sense for you while also meeting the needs of your clients. Share these hours in your canned presentation so buyers and sellers know what to expect.
- Attending state and national conventions are a great way to mix learning and networking with a vacation. Check these out a few times a year and get them on your calendar as soon as you can.
- Work-life balance is a must in real estate, especially because of the non-traditional hours. Take time to take care of yourself and spend time with your family. It's not selfish, it's called self-care.

Conclusion

If you've made it to the end of the book, you now have the skills and processes necessary to become a successful real estate agent.

You know the tips and tools to create the best you within a real estate setting. You also realize the importance of surrounding yourself with others who can make your business more profitable, and more enjoyable!

You also know what to do to become a major player in the industry. You understand the databases you must create to make this happen, as well as how to build relationships with people who can help your business grow.

You've learned the systems that can prompt you to constantly rise to the next level. This involves using the right listing approach for a particular seller and his or her property. It also requires knowing how to connect with your buyers and which open houses work best for which situations.

Finally—and perhaps most importantly—you recognize the importance of developing a level of balance. This keeps your real estate career a blessing versus turning it into a nightmare.

Good luck on your journey to becoming a sought-after and highly reputable real estate agent, a **Standout Agent**! God Bless.

-Cynthia

Recap

Now it's time to put into action all that you've learned. So here is your recap of steps:

- Reopen *You, Inc*
- Time vs money-decide how much of each you can dedicate
- What's your Why?
- Set goals
- Register for upcoming classes to educate yourself
- Write a business plan
- Name an accountability partner
- Study your competition
- Play hard to get
- Schedule everything as a calendar appointment
- Be easy
- Get used to rejection
- Solve problems with solutions
- Create a *wow* customer service experience
- Don't starve-find repeat customers
- Understand and communicate your value
- Get a mentor
- Consider a team

- Define your niche
- Build your database
- Get your Five a Day
- Create a VIP program
- Create an Influential Database
- Identify your closest 100
- Offer Surprise CMA's
- Build relationships and connect
- Utilize the power of donuts
- Target your marketing
- Create a social media plan
- Keep an eye on your online reputation
- Build your resume
- Throw away the recipe cards
- Research trends
- Delegate
- Understand who you are
- Set up your vendor team
- Fire customers when necessary-the right way!
- Build your canned presentations
- Create an Open House system
- Consider a VIP broker's open
- Invite nosy neighbors
- Find a door-knocking partner
- Always qualify buyers
- Name the house

- Show that you care
- Commit to never do one and done's again
- Organize your database
- Customize your follow up plan
- Schedule your time-both personal and professional
- Establish your business hours
- Attend conventions
- Do you have a work-life balance?

The conversation isn't over. I'd love for you to keep in touch. Tell me how your journey is coming along as a Standout Agent. Go to https://CynthiaDeLuca.com/ and send me a message under the contact button.

Want to keep in touch with other Standout Agents? Join the discussion on Facebook by joining the private group, **Standout Agents.**